JIRO
GASTRONOMY

まえがき

　この本には、『すきやばし次郎』の年間を通じてのすし種と、江戸前のにぎりずしの食べ方を紹介してあります。「鮨」は江戸時代、屋台の気軽な食べ物として発達してきました。鮨職人は握った鮨に「煮切り醬油」や「煮詰め」を引いて、客の前に置きました。客はそれを手で素早くつまんでは、茶を飲み、のれんで手を拭いて、屋台を後にしました。

　ですから、鮨を食べながらおしゃべりをしたり、酒を酌み交わすというのは、料理屋や居酒屋で、本来の鮨屋のあり方ではありません。『すきやばし次郎』はその「江戸前」を守って、出来たてのにぎりを美味しく召し上がっていただく「鮨屋」です。その評判が、今、世界中にいきわたり、連日、世界のあちこちからお客様がおいでになるようになりました。まことにありがたいことです。そのお客様や『次郎』の鮨に興味を持ってくださる方のために、この本を作りました。

　　　　　　　　　　　　　　　　　　　小野二郎 （すきやばし次郎）

Foreword

This book introduces readers to the sushi toppings served throughout the year at Sukiyabashi Jiro and some recommendations on how to fully enjoy Edo-style sushi. Sushi originated as casual food served at food stalls in the Edo era. Sushi chefs would brush "nikiri soy sauce" and "nitsume (or tsume) sauce" on top on the sushi they made and place them in front of customers. The customers would quickly eat the sushi with their hands, then drink some tea, wipe their hands on the noren curtain, and depart the food stall.

    Because of sushi's roots, conversing during the meal and sharing saké together, while fundamental to the origins of restaurants and pubs, is not customary to sushi houses. Sukiyabashi Jiro maintains the tradition of Edo-style sushi. We serve sushi that we want customers to enjoy as soon as they are prepared. Our reputation has spread, and now customers from around the world visit us every day. We are truly grateful. This book is dedicated to them and to everyone who has an interest in Sukiyabashi Jiro's sushi.

Jiro Ono Sukiyabashi JIRO

2	**まえがき** 小野二郎		Foreword	Jiro Ono

CHAPTER 1

7	**おまかせ図鑑**		**Omakase Tasting Menu**
9	かれい	………………	Karei
11	ひらめ	………………	Hirame
13	しんいか	………………	Shin-Ika
15	すみいか	………………	Sumi-Ika
17	いなだ	………………	Inada
19	しまあじ	………………	Shima-Aji
21	あかみ	………………	Akami
23	ちゅうとろ	………………	Chutoro
25	おおとろ	………………	Otoro
27	しんこ	………………	Shinko
29	こはだ	………………	Kohada
31	あわび	………………	Awabi
33	あじ	………………	Aji
35	くるまえび	………………	Kuruma-Ebi
37	とりがい	………………	Torigai
39	あかがい	………………	Akagai
41	かつお	………………	Katsuo
43	しゃこ	………………	Shako
45	さば	………………	Saba
47	たこ	………………	Tako
49	はまぐり	………………	Hamaguri
51	いわし	………………	Iwashi
53	さより	………………	Sayori
55	うに	………………	Uni
57	こばしら	………………	Kobashira
59	いくら	………………	Ikura
61	あなご	………………	Anago
63	かんぴょう巻き	………………	Kanpyo-Maki
65	おぼろ	………………	Oboro
67	たまご	………………	Tamago

CHAPTER 2

69	鮨を美味しく食べる		Eating Recipe
70	はじめに　山本益博	Introduction	Masuhiro Yamamoto
72	その1　手でつまむ　…………	Pick it up with your fingers	
74	その2　箸でつかむ　…………	Pick it up with your chopsticks	
76	その3　すし種を落とさず食べる　……	Avoid spilling the sushi topping	
78	その4　醬油をつける　…………	Flavor it with soy sauce	
80	その5　しょうがをつまむ　………	Eat some shoga	
81	その6　お茶を飲む　…………	Drink tea	
82	その7　醬油に浸さない　…………	Don't dip sushi rice into soy sauce	
	その8　甘いつめに醬油をつけない　…	Sweet tsume sauce	
83	その9　にぎりをひっくり返さない　…	Don't turn nigiri sushi upside down	
	その10　すし種をはがして食べない　…	Don't separate the sushi topping	
84	その11　ふたつにちぎって食べない　…	Don't break sushi into two	
	その12　鮨をためない　…………	Don't let sushi sit	

CHAPTER 3

87	**すきやばし次郎のトリセツ**	Dining at Jiro
88	予約………………………	Reservations
89	店を訪れる………………	Arriving at Sukiyabashi Jiro
91	「おまかせ」を食べる………	Enjoying our omakase tasting menu
92	ドレスコード………………	Dress code
	支払い……………………	Payment
95	見送り……………………	Visiting Sukiyabashi Jiro again
	住所………………………	Address

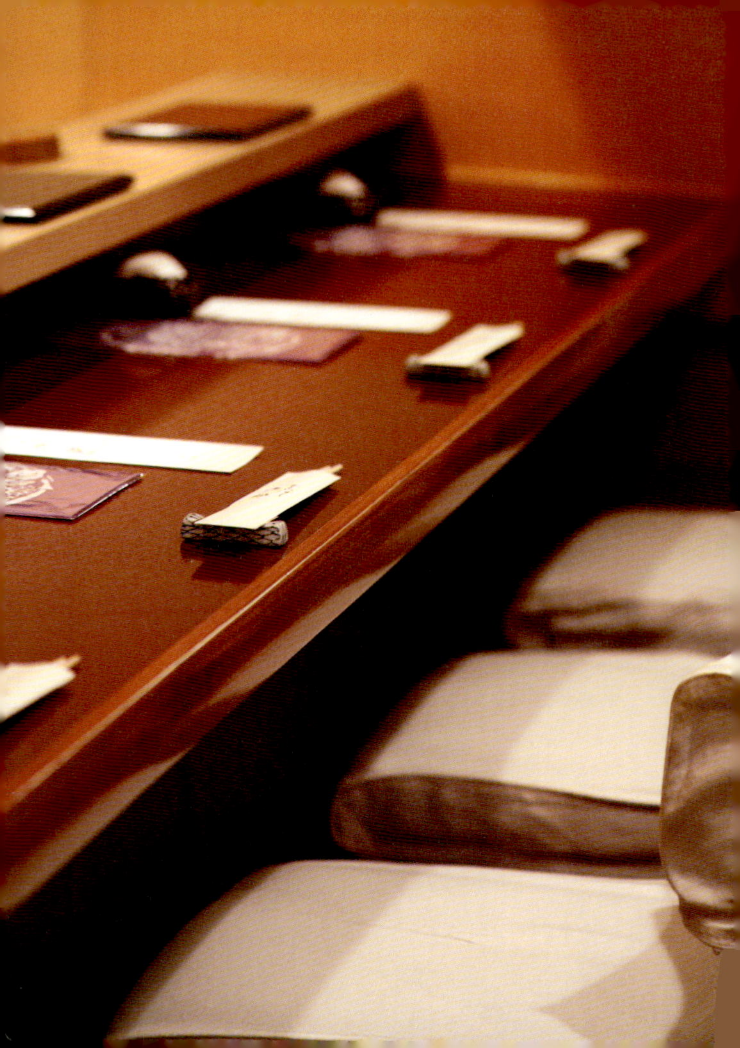

CHAPTER 1

おまかせ図鑑

Omakase Tasting Menu

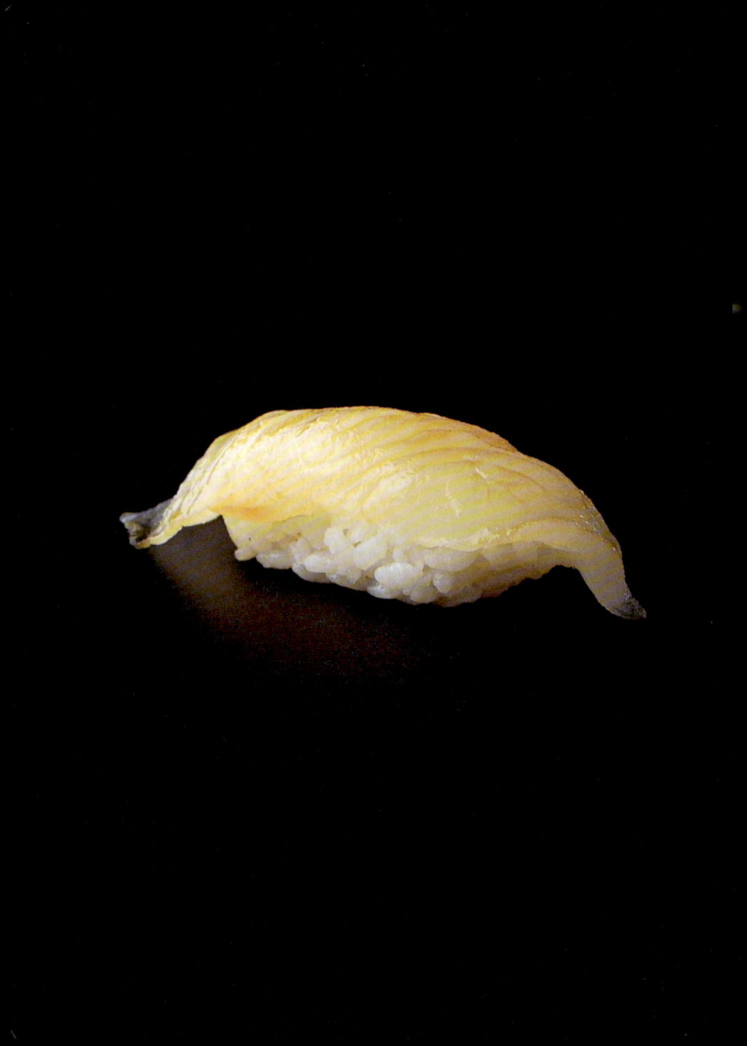

SUKIYABASHI JIRO's Tasting Menu

かれい

Karei : Sole

【鰈】 4月から10月：April - October

　白身から握るようになったのは『すきやばし次郎』が最初である。小野二郎が言う。「うちでは、まこがれいを使っていますが、身はひらめより堅いので、寝かせる時間もひらめより長いですよ。朝、河岸から仕入れたかれいを昼に出さなくてはならないときは、切り身を少し薄めにして切らないと、酢めしと一体にならないんです。淡白でしかも最初のにぎりということもあり、あとでもう一回握ってというお客様も多いです」

Sukiyabashi Jiro was the first sushi restaurant to serve whitefish to begin the omakase tasting menu. Jiro Ono says, *"We use makogarei (marbled sole). But because its flesh is tougher than hirame (flounder), we let it age for a longer time. If we procure karei from the market in the morning and have to serve it during the day, we slice it thinly. If we don't, it won't become one with the vinegared rice. Since its taste is mild, we often serve it as the course starter. There are many customers who order it as an encore."*

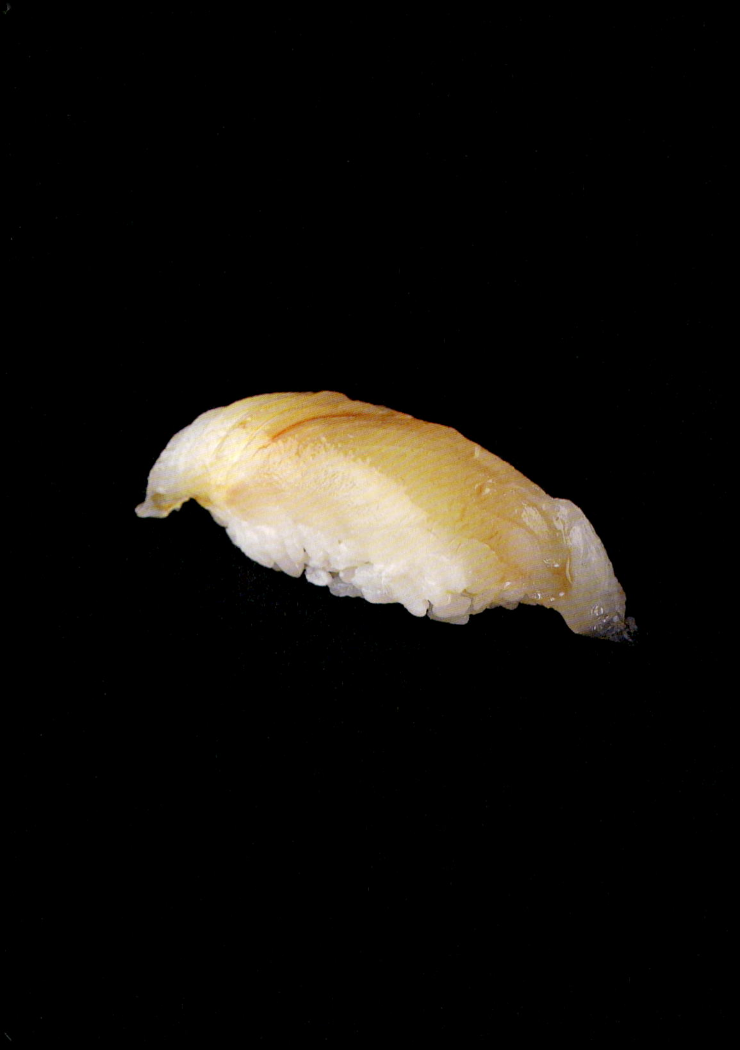

SUKIYABASHI JIRO's Tasting Menu

ひらめ

Hirame : Flounder

【鮃】 11月から3月：November - March

　ひらめは、たいと並んで冬の白身の魚の王様である。『次郎』では、おまかせコースの最初にこのひらめが握られる。昔ながらの江戸前の鮨屋では、「おまかせ」では、まぐろから握られるのが常だった。まぐろが、江戸前の鮨屋を代表するすし種であったからだ。それを、味の濃淡を考え、淡白な味わいのひらめから握るようになったのは『次郎』のオリジナルである。今では、多くの鮨屋がそれに倣っている。

Along with tai (sea bream), hirame is the king of winter whitefish. At Sukiyabashi Jiro, we serve hirame as the first item of our omakase tasting menu. At Edo-style sushi restaurants, sushi chefs used to maintain the tradition of beginning the meal with maguro (tuna). This was because maguro epitomizes Edo-style sushi. Mindful of the contrast between strong and mild flavors, at Sukiyabashi Jiro we serve gentle-tasting hirame first, an original idea. Today, many sushi restaurants have followed in our footsteps by adopting this practice.

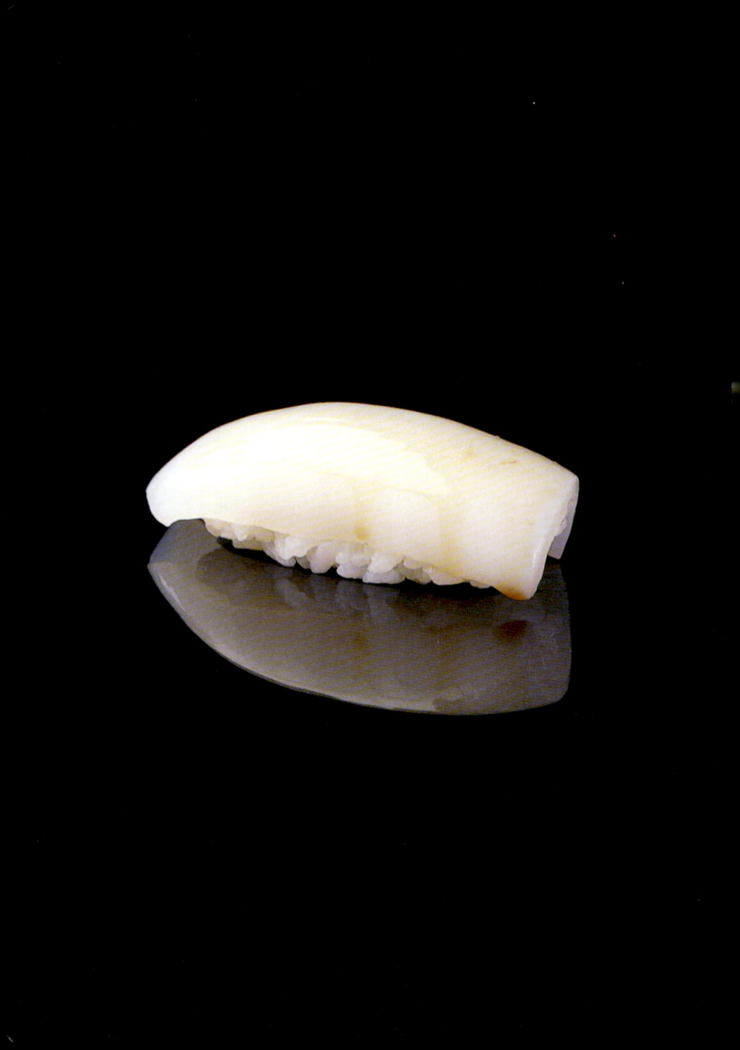

SUKIYABASHI JIRO's Tasting Menu

しんいか

Shin-Ika : Juvenile Cuttlefish

【新烏賊】 ７月から８月にかけて：July - August

　すみいかのこどもをしんいかと呼ぶ。こどもというより赤ん坊といったほうが正しいか。つやのある白い肌は、つるつるで、にぎりでいただくと舌を滑るような味わいが楽しい。二郎は次のように説明する。「しんこと違って、しんいかはどんなに小さくとも味があるんです。甘みがあって旨いいかです。小ぶりで１杯ちょうどのしんいかで握れる鮨がにぎりとしちゃ、いちばん旨いんじゃないですか」

Juvenile sumi-ika (cuttlefish) is called *"shin-ika." "Baby"* is perhaps the more apt term. Shin-ika has smooth, glossy white skin. When you eat it as sushi, its silky texture on your tongue is pure pleasure. Jiro explains, *"Unlike shinko (juvenile kohada), shin-ika is full of flavor, no matter how small it is. It is delicious because it is so savory. Sushi topped with a piece of small but flavorful shin-ika is the most delicious thing."*

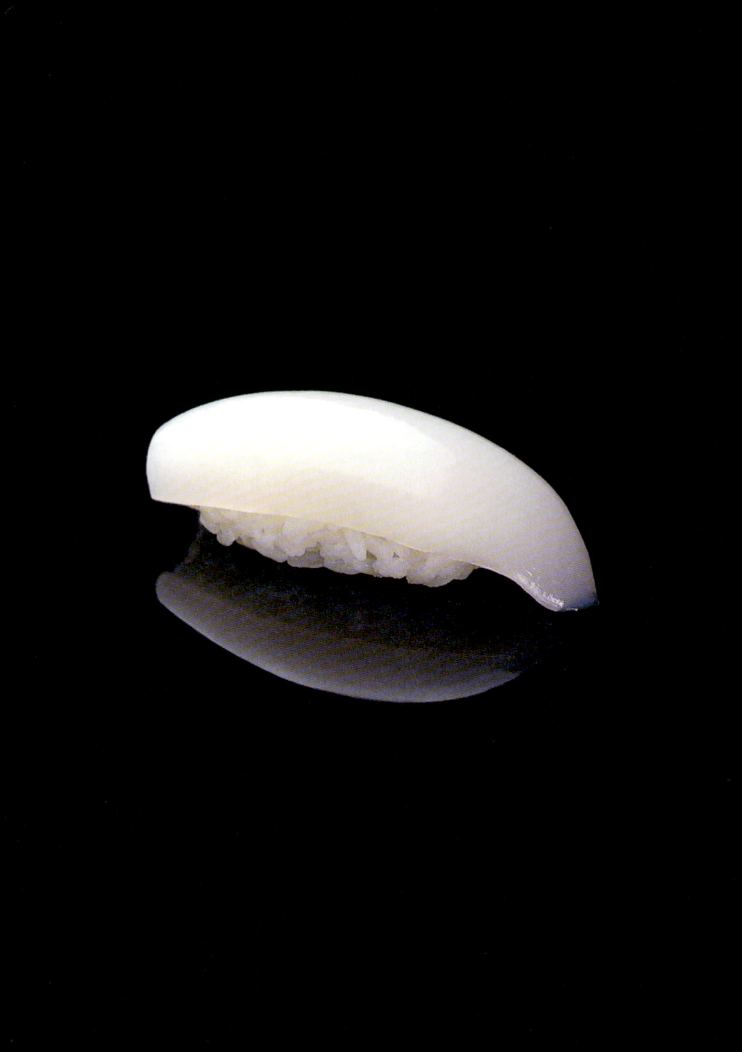

SUKIYABASHI JIRO's Tasting Menu   4

すみいか

Sumi-Ika : Golden Cuttlefish

【墨烏賊】 通年：All seasons

『次郎』は夏場、あおりいかをすし種として握ってきた。ところが、このところあおりいかが不漁で、ほとんど登場しなくなった。いま『次郎』でいかといえば、すみいかである。二郎が言う。「私の通うてんぷらの『みかわ』でも、いつもは見たこともないような立派なあおりいかのてんぷらを食べさせてくれますが、近ごろはすみいかですね。すみいかはいっとき痩せたもので出ますが、年中美味しいいかです」

At Sukiyabashi Jiro, the arrival of summer used to mean the appearance of aori-ika (bigfin reef squid) as a sushi topping. Nowadays, however, there are almost no opportunities for us to offer it due to poor catch. So when we serve ika, we serve sumi-ika. Jiro says, *"A tempura restaurant that I frequent, 'Mikawa,' served splendid tempura of aori-ika, the likes I've never seen before. But they are gone these days, and sumi-ika is offered instead. Sumi-ika has a skinny phase depending on the season, but it is delicious all year round."*

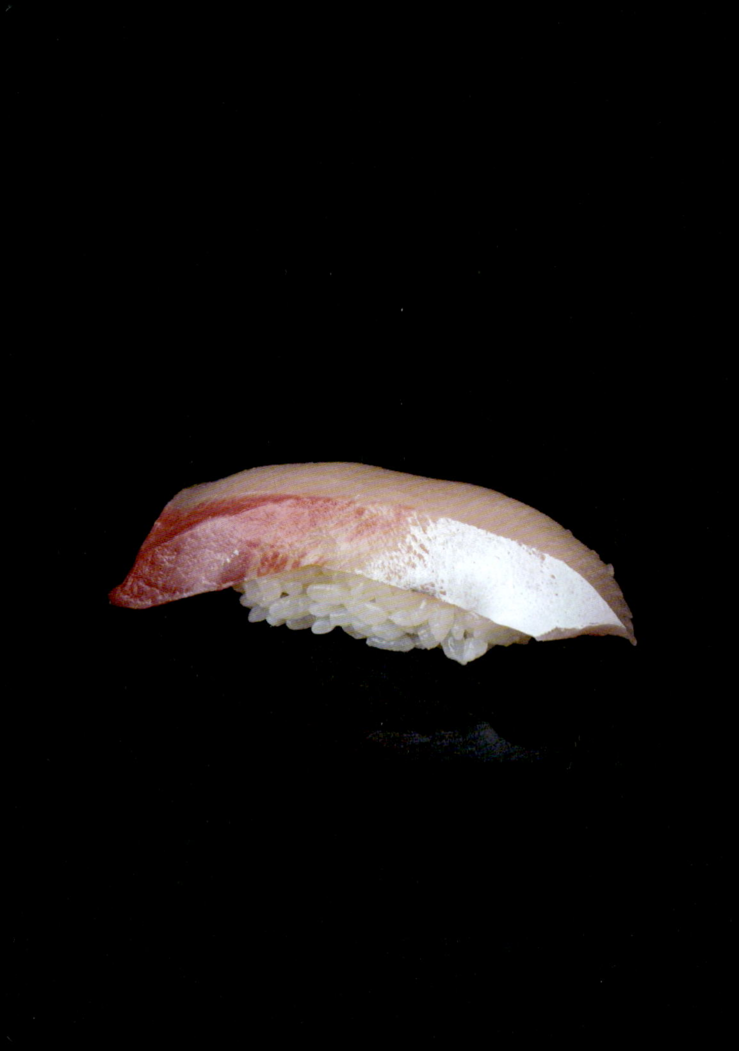

いなだ

Inada : Juvenile Yellowtail

【鰍】　通年：All seasons

　いなだはぶりの幼魚である。『次郎』では白身、いかのあと、「色物」として３番手に登場するすし種である。二郎は言う。「『色物』としてはほかに、しまあじ、かんぱちがありますが、このところいなだの出番が最も多いです。３年ほど前から冬のすし種としてぶりを使うようになり、いなだはやや影が薄くなった感がありますが、ぶりほど脂は乗っていませんが、すっきりとした味わいが持ち味ですね」

Inada is juvenile buri (yellowtail). At Sukiyabashi Jiro, inada makes its entrance as a *"colored"* topping, third in order after whitefish and ika (cuttlefish). Jiro says, *"Besides inada, shima-aji (yellow jack) and kanpachi (greater amberjack) can be used as 'colored toppings.' These days, however, we turn to inada most often. We began using buri as a winter topping three years ago. We felt that inada would be overpowered by other toppings. But because it is not as fatty as buri, it has a clean, distinct flavor."*

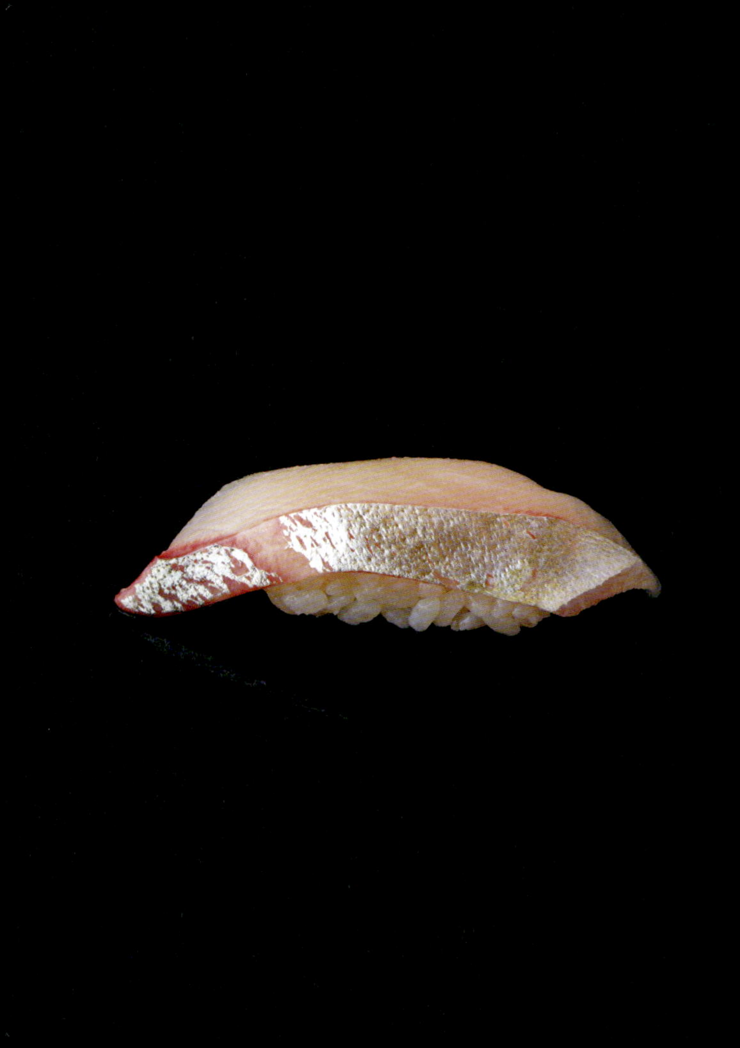

SUKIYABASHI JIRO's Tasting Menu

しまあじ

Shima-Aji : Yellow Jack

【縞鯵】　夏：Summer

『次郎』では、養殖物、冷凍物の魚は一切使わない。しまあじももちろん天然物である。これが、養殖物とは段違いの香りと味わい。誰しもが、潮のほのかな香りと、嚙み応えのある身質に目を丸くする。ところが、このしまあじが、いま河岸に滅多に入らない。あっても１〜２枚。さほどに、いまや活けのしまあじは幻の魚になりつつある。夏のおまかせでしまあじが出てきたら、かなりの幸運と言ってよい。

At Sukiyabashi Jiro, we never use farmed fish or frozen fish. So our shima-aji is, of course, wild-caught. It has a fragrance and taste completely different from farmed shima-aji. Our customers become wide-eyed in amazement when they catch the subtle aroma of the ocean in our shima-aji and bite into its firm flesh. However, shima-aji are seldom found in fish markets these days – only one or two, if at all. Even more illusory are shima-aji delivered chilled to the restaurant with its freshness and quality maintained. You are in for a treat if shima-aji makes an appearance in the summer omakase tasting menu.

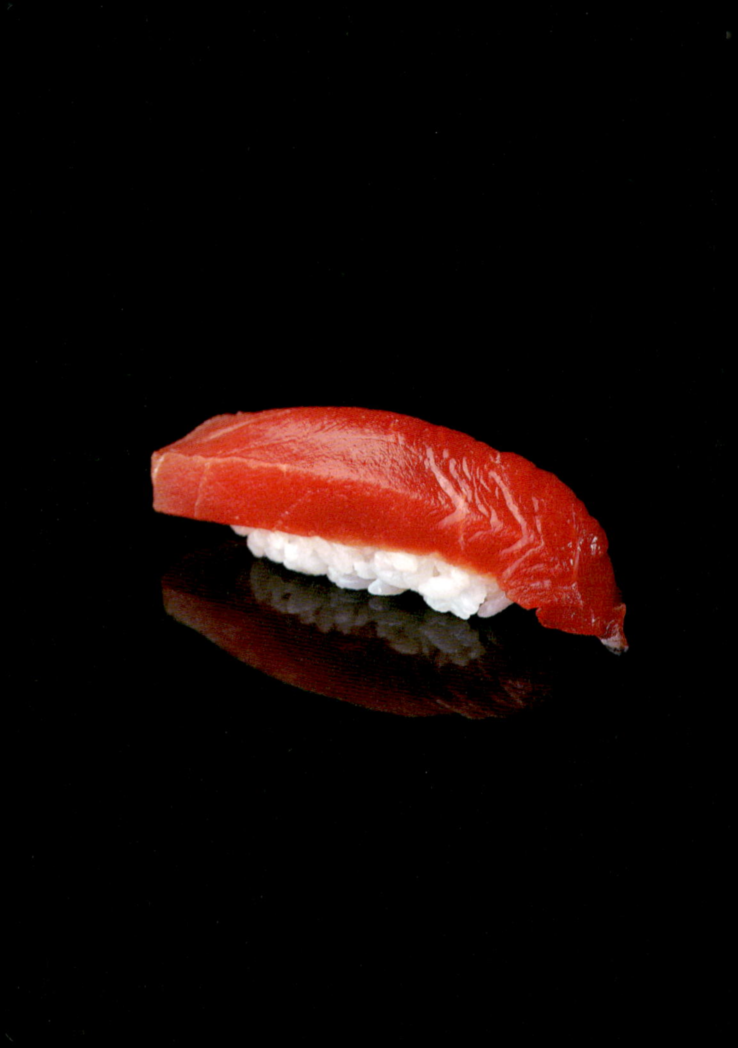

SUKIYABASHI JIRO's Tasting Menu

あかみ

Akami : Lean Bluefin Tuna

【鮪赤身】 通年：All seasons

　あかみとはまぐろの赤身のことである。いまから150年以上前の江戸時代は、冷蔵設備が整っていなかったので、大きなまぐろの脂身（トロ）は使わず、赤身の塊を醬油樽の中に漬けて保存し、これを「づけ」と呼んだ。『次郎』では、予約に合わせて人数分をその都度「づけ」にする。二郎いわく「まぐろの赤身の酸味と醬油の相性がいいんです。こはだと並んで『江戸前』のにぎりの横綱ですね」。

Akami is the lean flesh of maguro (tuna). During the Edo era, over one hundred fifty years ago, there was no refrigeration. Consequently, the fatty sections (toro) of maguro were not consumed but removed and thrown away. Cuts of akami were preserved by marinating them in casks of soy sauce. This technique is called *"zuke."* At Sukiyabashi Jiro, we prepare zuke of akami for each of our reserved guests in advance. Jiro says, *"The acidity of akami and the savoriness of soy sauce are a perfect match. Together with kohada (gizzard shad), akami represents the pinnacle of Edo-style sushi."*

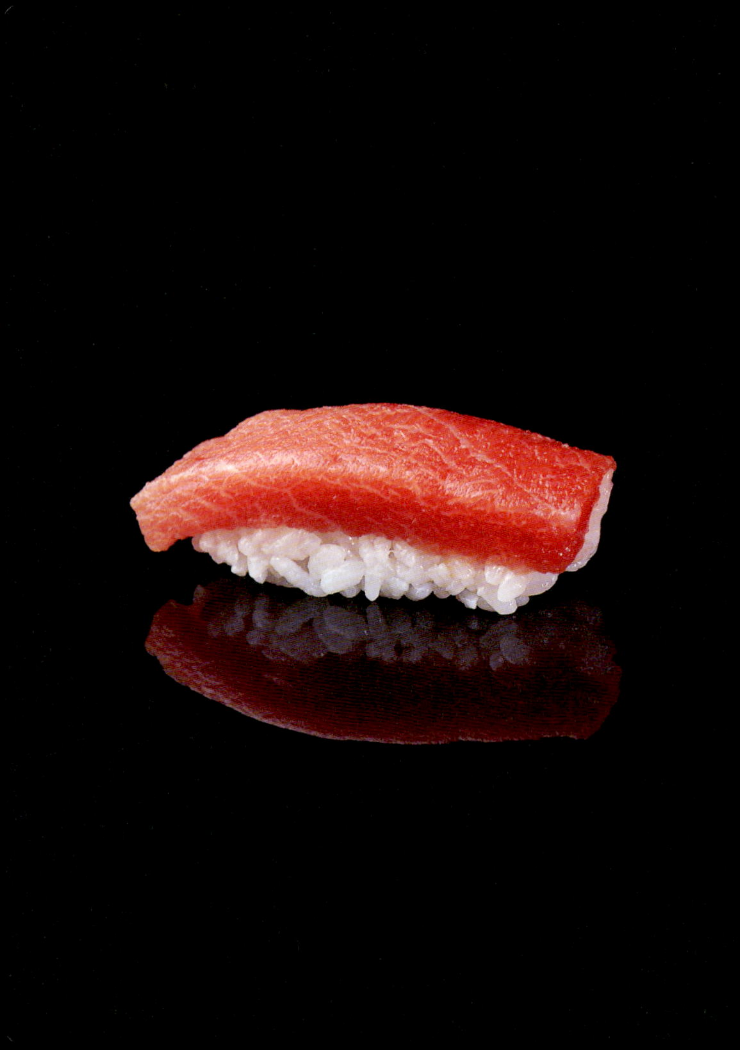

SUKIYABASHI JIRO's Tasting Menu

ちゅうとろ
Chutoro : Medium Fatty Bluefin Tuna

【鮪ちゅうとろ】　通年：All seasons

「まぐろではあかみ、ちゅうとろ、おおとろとありますが、旨みの点で言えばちゅうとろが一番じゃないでしょうか。握るときに手でつかんだ瞬間、脂の乗りがすぐにわかります。どこまで、寝かせて熟成させるか、それが腕ですね。そのために、毎日味見を欠かしません」。『次郎』ではもちろん、生のまぐろしか握らない。「まぐろがないとのれんを出せませんので、いま一番の悩みの種と言っていいでしょうか」

Jiro says, *"Maguro consists of akami, chutoro, and otoro. When it comes to umami, nothing beats chutoro. The moment you grasp it in your hand to make its sushi, you can tell immediately how fatty it is. Aging chutoro takes skills. That's why it is essential to sample it every day."* At Sukiyabashi Jiro, we of course only use fresh maguro. Jiro says, *"A day without maguro means a day a sushi restaurant can't open for business. Right now, it is the most worrisome sushi topping."*

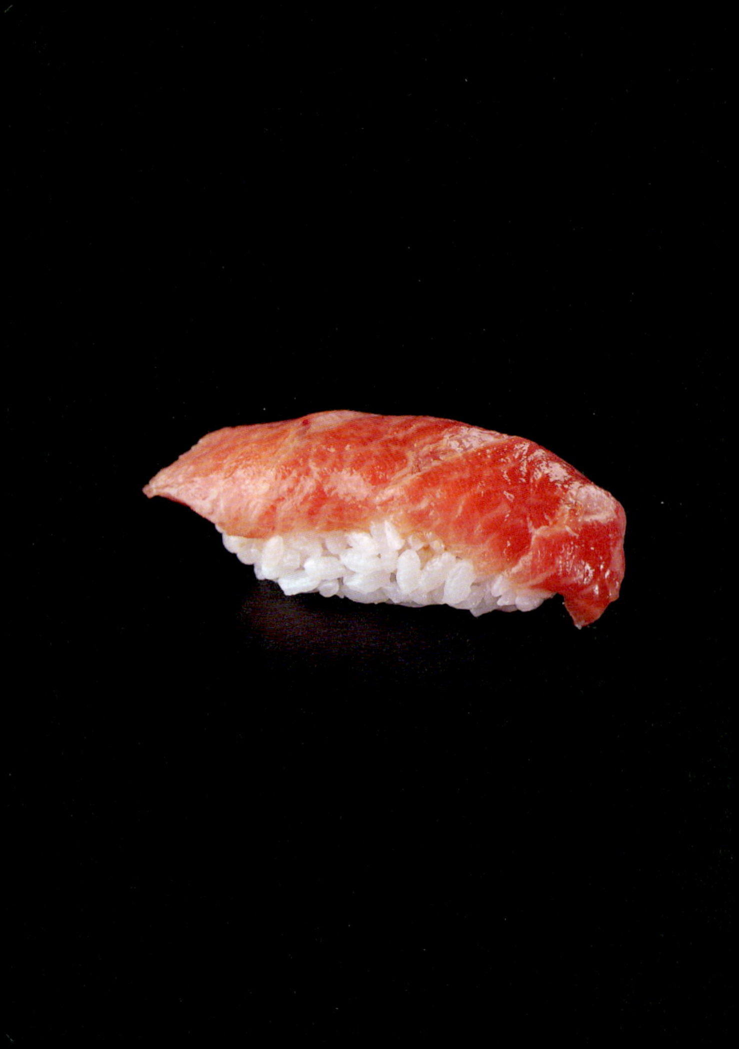

おおとろ
Otoro : Fatty Bluefin Tuna

【鮪おおとろ】　通年：All seasons

『次郎』のまぐろは築地の仲買『フジタ』から仕入れてくる。おおとろといえども脂が乗っているより、香りを重視したまぐろが『次郎』ではお好みで、その嗜好が同じらしい。小野二郎は言う。「いいまぐろを握っているときほど、気持ちのよいものはありません。その反対に、いいまぐろがなかったときは気が気じゃありません。大間のまぐろがいいといわれますが、本当にいいまぐろは大間といえども100本に1本あるかないかの程度じゃないでしょうか」

Sukiyabashi Jiro's maguro (tuna) is procured by the Tsukiji broker Fujita. Even for otoro, we desire maguro to be fragrant more than being merely fatty. This preference is also shared by Fujita. Jiro Ono says, *"There is no better feeling in the world than making sushi with good maguro. On the other hand, if we can't procure good maguro, we feel quite uneasy. They say that good maguro comes from Oma, Aomori. But even in Oma, only one out of one hundred maguro meets our standards."*

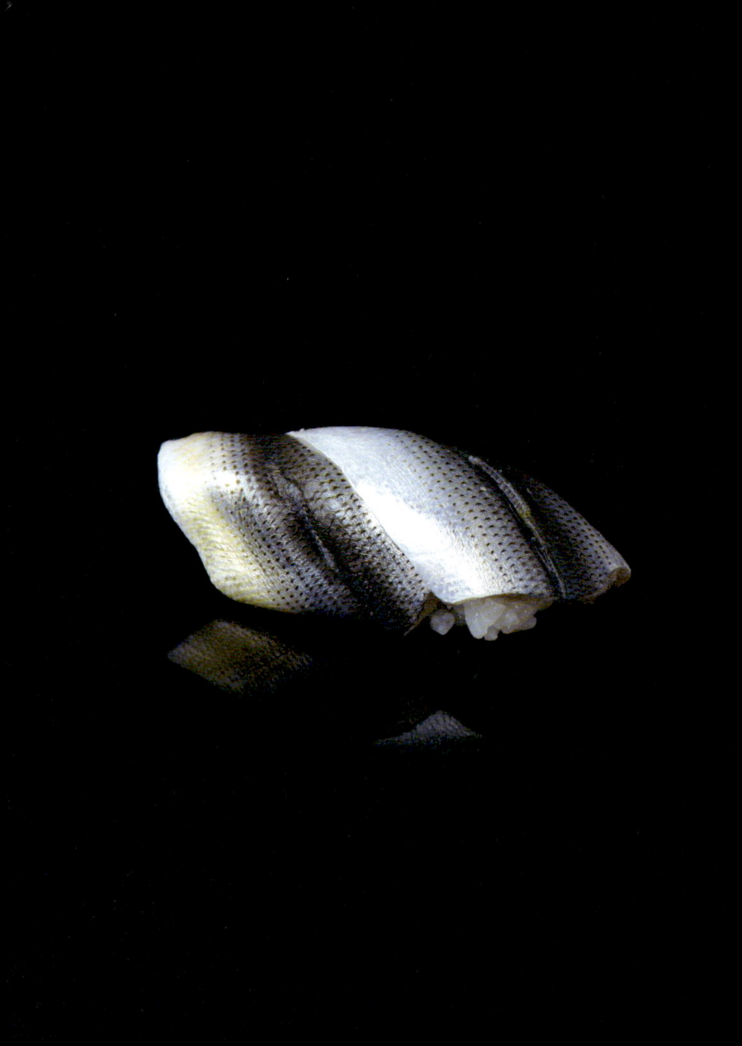

SUKIYABASHI JIRO's Tasting Menu **10**

しんこ

Shinko : Juvenile Gizzard Shad

【新子】 7月末から8月：End of July - August

　しんこは、こはだの幼魚。ほんの一時だけ握られる。一昔前まで、こはだは秋から春にかけてが旬で、春から夏場にかけてはあじが「ひかりもの」の主役だった。それが、輸送手段と保冷設備の格段の進歩で、こはだもあじも一年中出回るようになった。二郎が言う。「しんこは二枚づけにして握りますが、手間を食べているようなものです。でも、季節を感じさせるネタとしては夏に欠かせませんね」

Shinko is juvenile gizzard shad. In the past, it held the starring role as the *"silver-skinned fish"* in season from fall to spring, as aji (horse mackerel) did from spring to summer. As delivery and refrigeration technologies advanced, kohada and aji became available year-round. Jiro says, *"We place two marinated shinko on the sushi rice. You can taste the time and effort involved. Still, nothing beats shinko as the topping that offers the taste of summer."*

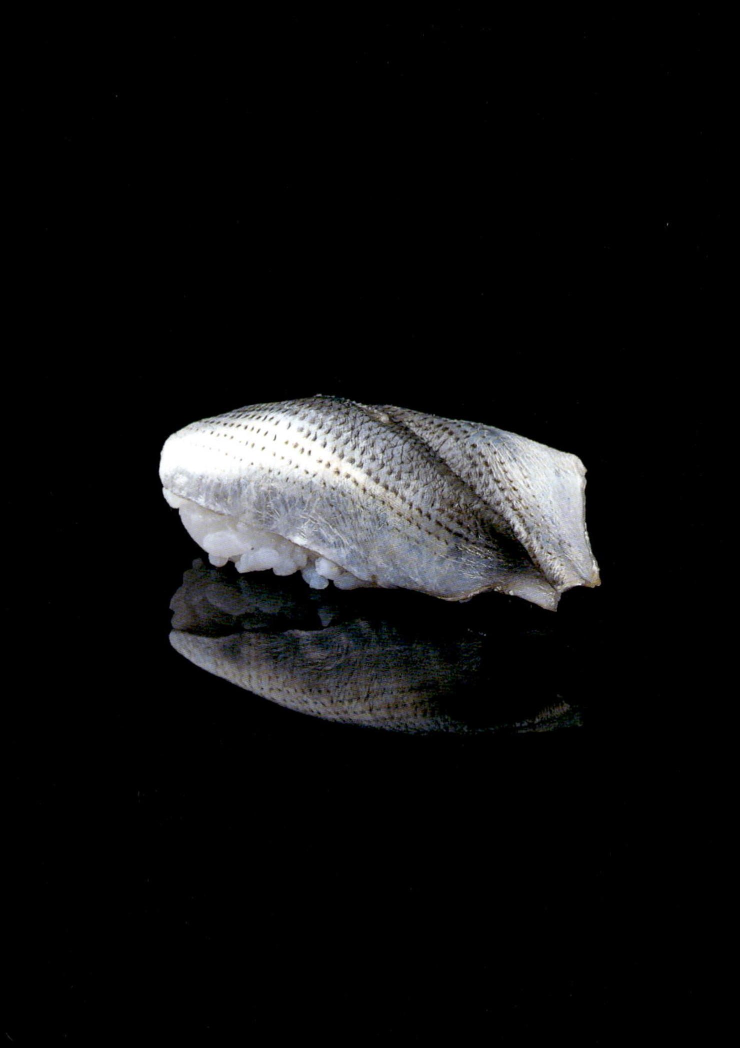

SUKIYABASHI JIRO's Tasting Menu

こはだ

Kohada : Gizzard Shad

【小鰭】 通年：All seasons

「『次郎』で最も大切なすし種は何でしょうか？」の問いに小野二郎は「こはだ」と即答した。「こはだがうまくできなきゃ鮨屋はのれんが出せません。旨みが出るまでしっかり締めますが、生のときはわからずに酢締めにしたあと、石油くささが残っているときがある。それはすべて処分します。ですから、厄介な魚なんです」。『次郎』はこのこはだを少し斜めにひねって握る。「私が考えました。女の子座りのこはだのにぎりです」

When asked *"What is the most important sushi topping at Sukiyabashi Jiro?"* Jiro Ono immediately replies, *"Kohada."* He continues, *"Kohada makes or breaks a sushi chef. Incredible flavor is created by marinating it in vinegar. But some kohada may develop an odor of heavy oil during this process. We discard all of those kohada. This is why it is such a troublesome fish."* At Sukiyabashi Jiro, we place kohada diagonally on the sushi rice. Jiro says, *"I invented this style. It is kohada imitating a feminine sitting pose."*

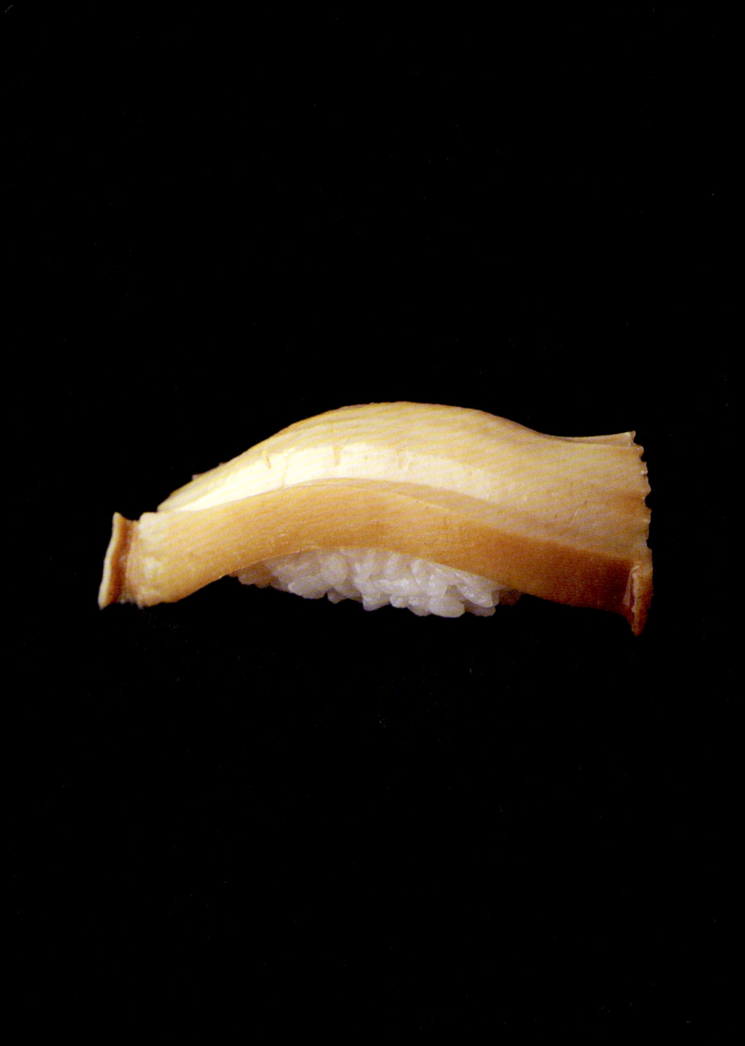

SUKIYABASHI JIRO's Tasting Menu

あわび

Awabi : Abalone

【鮑】 5月から9月：May - September

　あわびは夏の貝の王様。すし種としては生では握らない。『次郎』では、硬くならず、磯の香りを活かすために、水と酒で3〜4時間煮る。そして、そのまま煮汁につけて冷ます。あわびはとても握りにくいすし種で、そのために包丁を小刻みにアール（湾曲）に入れて切る。質の高いあわびなら、切っただけで香りが漂うほど。「最近になって、温めてから握るようになりました」

Awabi is the king of summer shellfish. As a sushi topping, it is not served raw. At Sukiyabashi Jiro, we simmer it in saké and water for three to four hours, releasing the fragrance of the seashore without toughening the flesh. The awabi is then left to cool in its broth. Because awabi is difficult to handle when making sushi, we would score it with a series of small curves. High-quality awabi will release its scent simply upon being cut. Jiro says, *"These days, however, we just warm awabi when preparing sushi."*

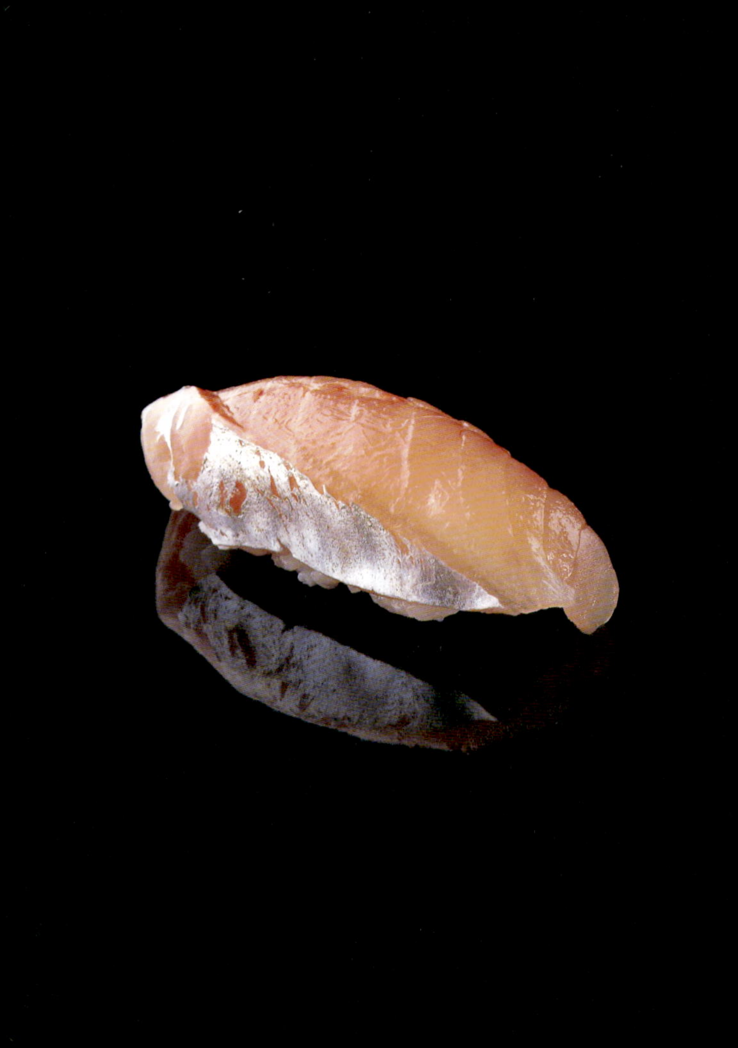

SUKIYABASHI JIRO's Tasting Menu 13

あじ

Aji : Japanese Horse Mackerel

【鯵】 通年：All seasons

　あじは生で握られるが、昔は酢締めといって、酢と塩で調味してすし種とした。小野二郎は言う。「築地から買ってきたら、まず初めに手をつける（下拵え）のがあじ。内臓を素早く取り除き、すぐに氷水で洗い、冷蔵庫へ入れます。こうすると、鮮度も落ちないし、生ぐささも出ません」。まぐろのあとに握っても、誰もが一様に驚きの声を上げ、一通り食べたあとの「もうひとつ」でも一番人気があじだという。

Aji is served raw for sushi. But in past, it was prepared by marinating in salt and vinegar (sujime). *"When the catch is brought back from Tsukiji,"* Jiro Ono says, *"the first fish I lay my hands on are aji. I promptly remove their innards, then immediately wash them in ice water and place them in the refrigerator. This keeps aji's freshness, and prevents the raw odor of fish from forming."* The flavor of Sukiyabashi Jiro's aji shines through even when it is served after maguro (tuna), a rich fish. At the end of the omakase tasting menu, diners exclaim, *"One more aji!"*, making it the most popularly requested encore item.

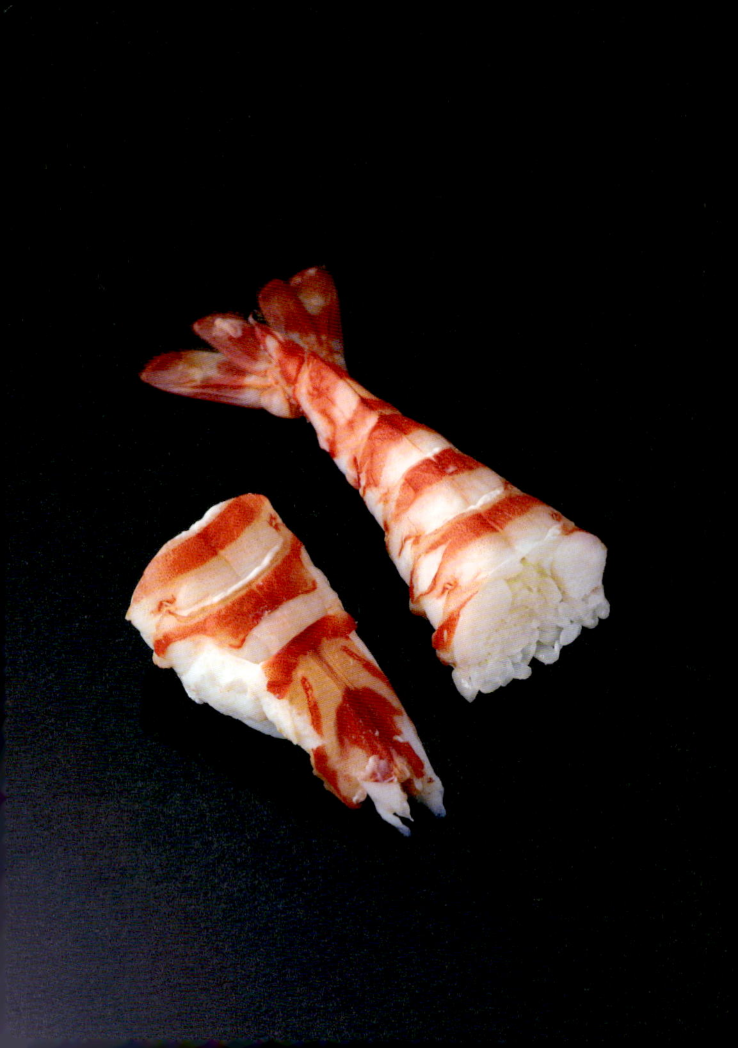

SUKIYABASHI JIRO's Tasting Menu 14

くるまえび

Kuruma-Ebi : Japanese Tiger Prawn

【車海老】 通年：All seasons

　いまでは、あちこちの鮨屋で、くるまえびを握る寸前に茹で上げるようになったが、それを最初に始めたのは『すきやばし次郎』で、いまから25年前のことである。小野二郎が言う。「夏場が美味しいですね。茹でたてを少しだけ冷まして握ることで、えびのみそを楽しんでいただけるようになりました。でも、このみそをはみださずに握るのがむずかしい。水分が多いから、握るとき滑ってしまうんです」

These days, there are many sushi restaurants that boil kuruma-ebi just before preparing it in sushi. Actually, Sukiyabashi Jiro originated this practice 25 years ago. Jiro Ono says, *"Kuruma-ebi are delicious in the summer. By letting them cool just a bit before using them in sushi, we allow their 'miso' (innards) to be enjoyed by our customers. However, topping them on sushi rice without the miso coming out is difficult. Because they have a high water content, they slip out of our hands."*

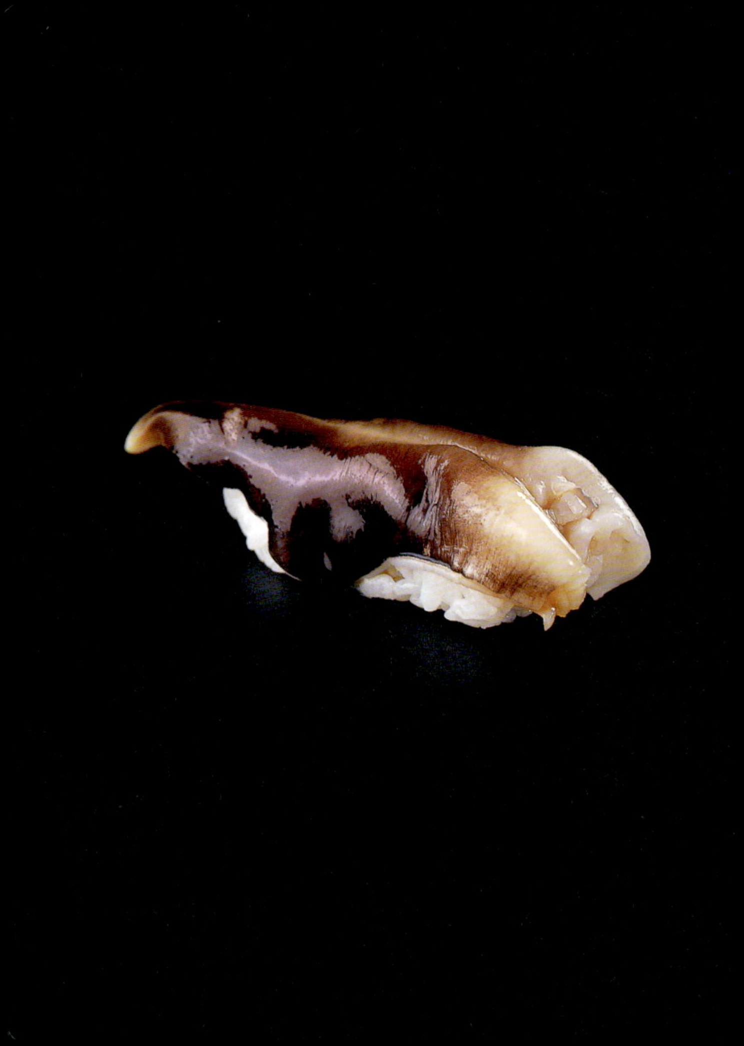

SUKIYABASHI JIRO's Tasting Menu

とりがい
Torigai : Cockle

【鳥貝】 4月から5月：April - May

　とりがいこそは春を告げる貝と呼んでいい。ただし、初夏にはあっという間に姿を消してしまうほどはかない旬の二枚貝である。

　小野二郎が言う。「昔は東京湾で見事なとりがいがいくらでも獲れたんです。江戸前のはまず、色つやが違う、大きさも違う。大きくて厚みもあるのに、柔らかいし、甘みも強い。とりがいは、季節を感じさせるネタですから、春の『おまかせ』には絶対欠かせない貝ですね」

Torigai can be called the shellfish that announces spring. But it is a strictly seasonal bivalve mollusk that disappears the moment summer starts. Jiro Ono says, *"A long time away, you could find endless amounts of splendid torigai in Tokyo Bay. This torigai has a different luster and size from others. Even though it is big and thick, it is soft and very sweet. Because torigai is a sushi topping that allows you to feel the season, it is an absolutely essential shellfish for our springtime omakase tasting menu."*

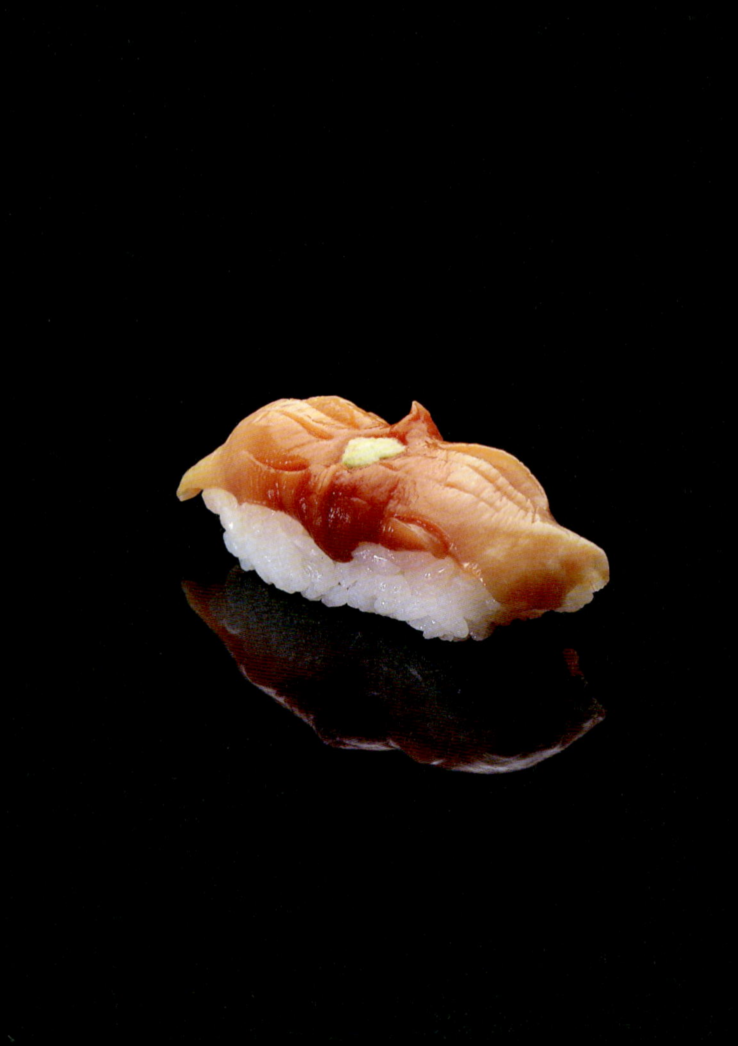

SUKIYABASHI JIRO's Tasting Menu 16

あかがい

Akagai : Red Clam

【赤貝】 通年：All seasons

　戦後、赤貝は東京湾で獲れなくなると、宮城の閖上（ゆりあげ）から届く赤貝が最上等品となった。ところが、東北大震災で閖上の赤貝が全滅、しかたなく東京以南の大分、香川あたりからのものを使うようになった。二郎は言う「赤貝は貝殻をむいてみるまで中の状態が判断できないむずかしい貝です。貝は、えびやかにの類と同じで、なんてったって鮮度が命です。うちではそのまま握ってお出ししています」

After the Second World War, akagai could no longer be found in Tokyo Bay. Akagai delivered from Yuriage in Miyagi Prefecture became the highest-quality akagai in Japan. However, the region's akagai were wiped out by the 2011 Tohoku earthquake and tsunami. As a result, those from Oita and Kagawa, came to be used. Jiro Ono says, *"Akagai are notoriously difficult shellfish to use. You can't tell their quality until you shuck them. Like shrimp and crab, shellfish must be fresh above all else. At Sukiyabashi Jiro, we serve akagai straight out of their shells."*

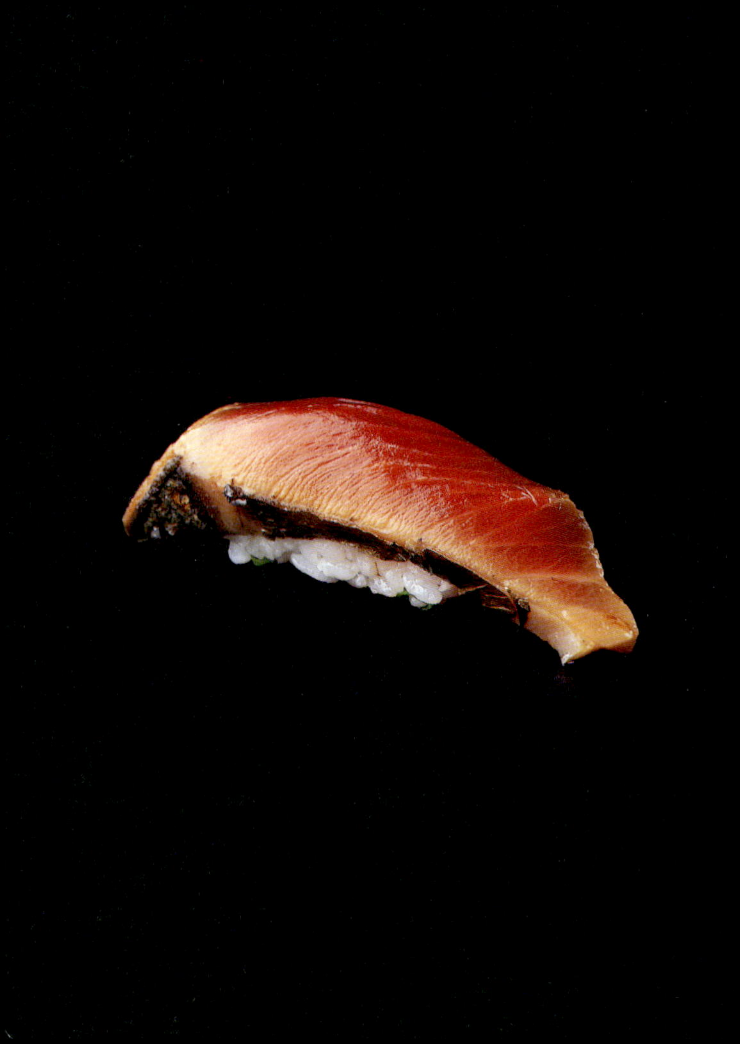

SUKIYABASHI JIRO's Tasting Menu

かつお

Katsuo : Skipjack Tuna

【鰹】 6月から11月：June - November

　かつおは厄介な魚で、見た目ではなかなか良し悪しがわからない。おろしてはじめて脂の乗り具合などがわかる。『次郎』では三枚におろした身を藁であぶる。焼き魚にせず、皮目を優しく焼き上げるためだ。そして、すぐに冷凍庫へ。二郎いわく「氷水に浸けては、せっかくの皮と身の間の脂が流れてしまうから。藁でいぶしたかつおのにぎりは、香り高く旨みが濃く、外国のお客様にもとても好評です」。

Katsuo is a vexing fish. At first glance, it's hard to tell if you've caught a good fish or bad. It is only after you fillet it that its fattiness is revealed. At Sukiyabashi Jiro, we roast three fillets over burning straw, so as to lightly grill the skin without cooking the flesh. The fish is then immediately placed in the freezer. Jiro says, *"If grilled katsuo is soaked in cold water, the precious fat between the skin and the flesh flows away. Nigiri of katsuo smoked over straw is fragrant and rich in savory flavor. They are popular with our international guests."*

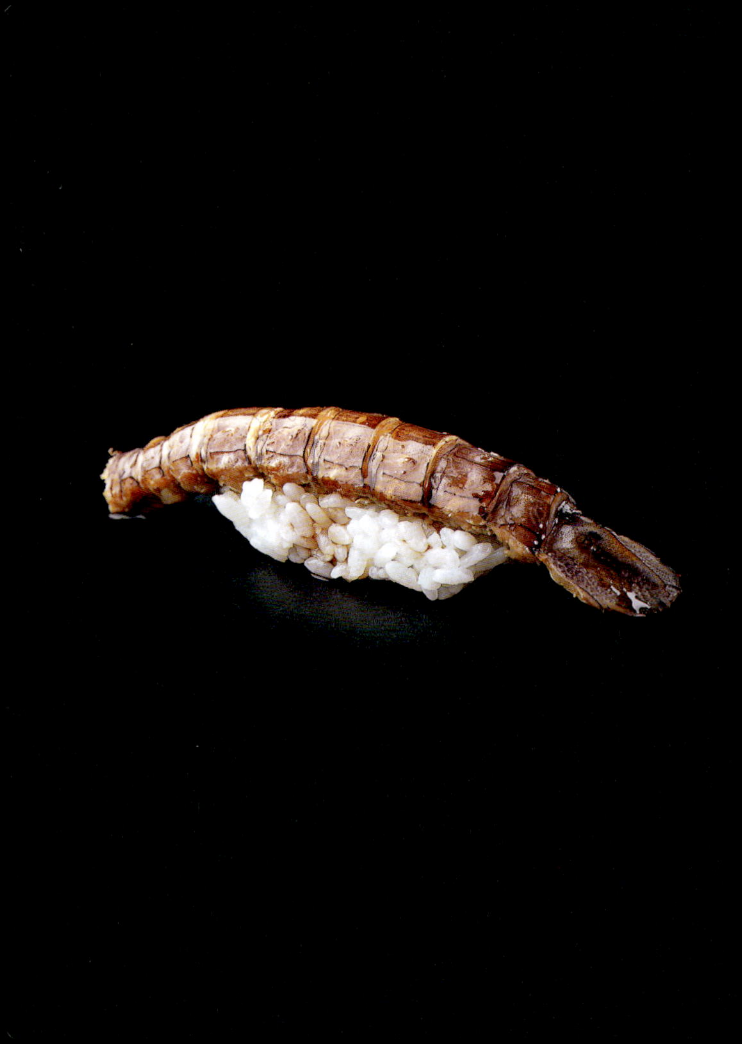

SUKIYABASHI JIRO's Tasting Menu 18

しゃこ

Shako : Mantis Shrimp

【蝦蛄】 6月から10月：June - October

『次郎』では、しゃこはかつおのすぐ後に登場する。なぜか。『次郎』のかつおは藁でいぶされているため、後味がしばらく残る。残り香は嬉しいが、次のにぎりにとっては邪魔物である。かつおの香りを一気に消し去り、その瞬間に旨みが口中にあふれるのが漬け込みの子持ちのしゃこ。これが、逆の順番だと双方の味が台無しになる。『次郎』では、かつおあってのしゃこと呼びたいほど、初夏からの絶妙のコンビ。

At Sukiyabashi Jiro, shako makes its entrance immediately after katsuo (skipjack tuna). Because we roast katsuo over burning straw at Sukiyabashi Jiro, the fish's aftertaste remains. While a lingering flavor is generally delightful, it interferes with the taste of sushi to come. Roe-bearing shako, cooked and then steeped in broth, completely cleanses the palate of the flavor of katsuo. At the same time, its rich flavor blooms in your mouth. If the order of katsuo and shako were reversed, both flavors would be wasted. At Sukiyabashi Jiro, katsuo and shako are a match made in heaven from the early summer.

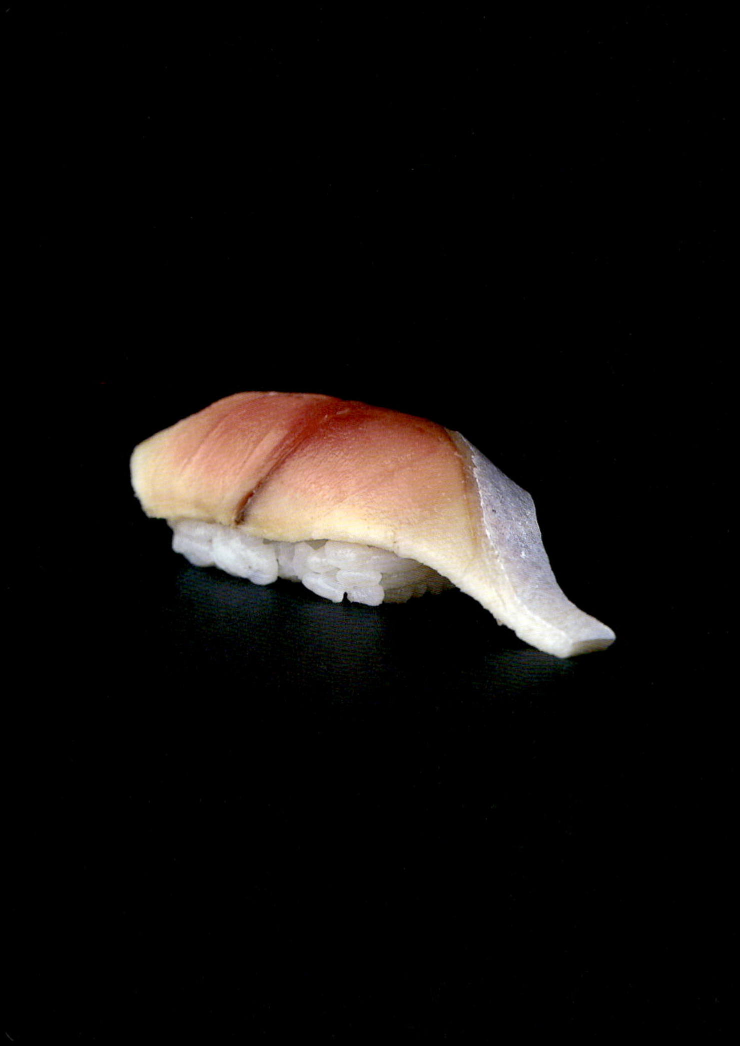

SUKIYABASHI JIRO's Tasting Menu

さば

Saba : Mackerel

【鯖】 11月から3月頃：November - March

　ロンドンの『ザ・ファット・ダック』のオーナーシェフ、ヘストン・ブルメンタールが『次郎』のカウンターで「私はさばが世界でいちばん大好き」と言いながら『次郎』の舌に差し込むような旨み十分の締めさばのにぎりを食べて絶句してしまった。小野二郎が言う。「締め方が甘いとさばの旨みは十分に出てきません。うちでは1週間ほど酢締めにします。外国の方にとても喜ばれます」

Sitting at the counter of Sukiyabashi Jiro, Heston Blumenthal, the owner-chef of The Fat Duck in London, said, *"Saba is my favorite food in the world."* As he bit into Sukiyabashi Jiro's absolutely savory vinegared saba sushi, he was at a loss for words. Jiro Ono says, *"If vinegared saba is not properly prepared, the fish's rich flavor is not fully exposed. We actually marinate our saba in vinegar for about a week. This delectable fish is highly popular with our international customers."*

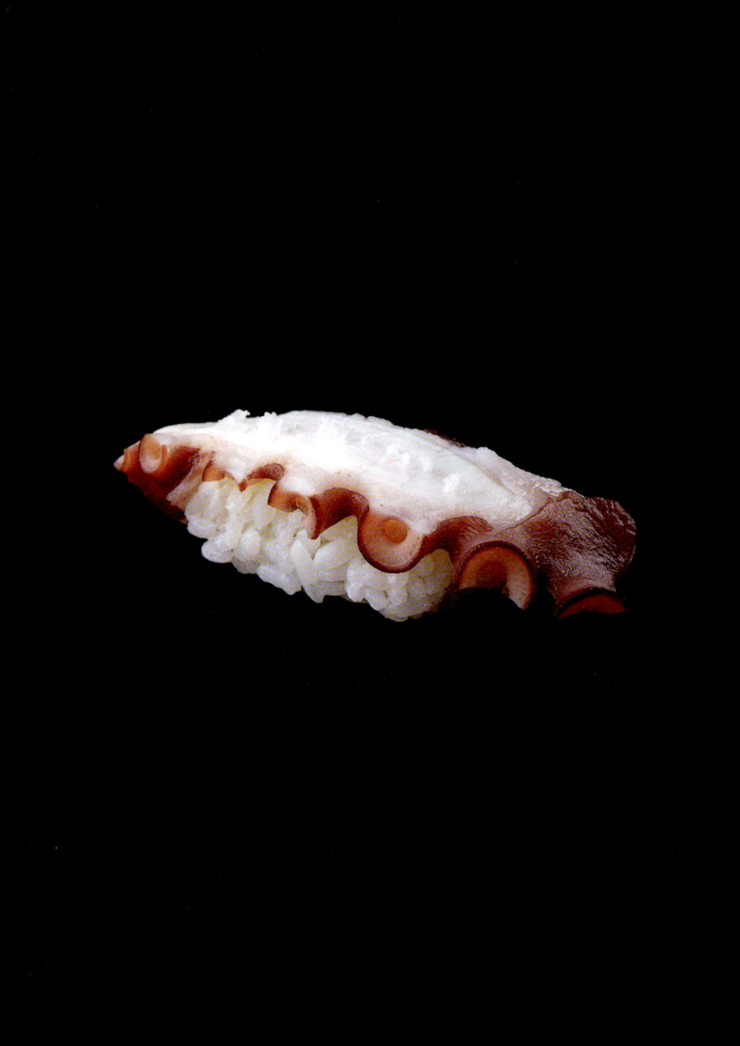

SUKIYABASHI JIRO's Tasting Menu 20

たこ
Tako : Octopus

【蛸】1月、2月：January - February

　どの鮨屋でもたこは通年あるが、『次郎』では、真冬に初めて登場する。フランス料理の名匠ジョエル・ロブションが「たこはどこで食べてもゴムを嚙んでいるようで、旨くもなんともなく、苦手なんだ」と言いながら食べ、「ラングースト（伊勢えび）の味がする！」と感嘆の声をあげた。たこは甲殻類をえさとするが、1時間揉んで、その味と香りを引き出した『次郎』のたこは、冬のスペシャリテである。

At other sushi restaurants, tako is served year-round. At Sukiyabashi Jiro, however, tako first makes its appearance in midwinter. Joël Robuchon, the master French chef, said, ***"Whenever I'm eating octopus, it feels like I'm chewing rubber. It doesn't taste good, and I have a hard time with it."*** But the moment he tried Sukiyabashi Jiro's tako, he exclaimed, ***"It tastes like lobster!"*** When preparing tako, we knead its flesh for one hour, releasing its fragrance and flavor. It tastes as if its diet consists purely of crustaceans like shrimp and lobster. At present, tako is Sukiyabashi Jiro's winter specialty.

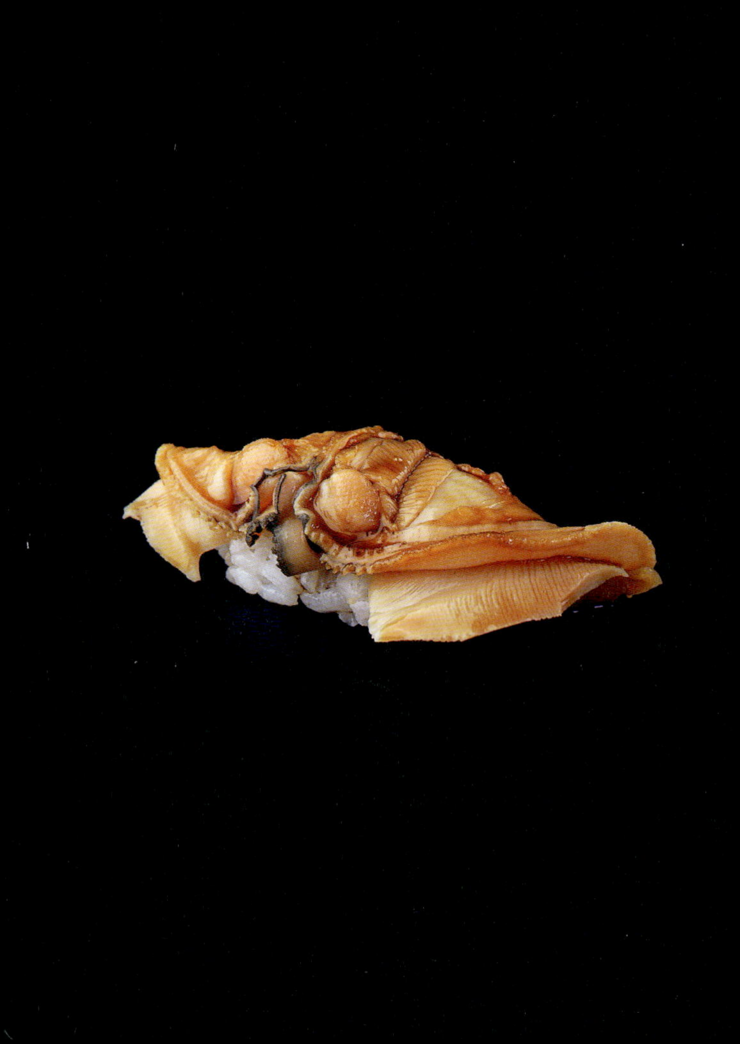

SUKIYABASHI JIRO's Tasting Menu 21

はまぐり

Hamaguri : Clam

【蛤】 11月から3月頃：November - March

　はまぐりは、遠浅の海にすむ二枚貝で、江戸時代から、いまの東京湾で盛んに獲れた。したがって、はまぐりは、まぐろ、こはだ、あなごなどと並ぶ、江戸前のにぎりずしの古典である。小野二郎が言う。「貝は、煮るとすぐに硬くなるので、短時間に火を通し、その煮汁に砂糖、醤油などの調味料を加えたものに漬け込んで、味を調えます」。甘くてジューシーな味わいのはまぐりが、酢めしにとてもよく合う。

Hamaguri is a bivalve mollusk inhabiting the shoals of the sea. Since the Edo era, it has been found in great abundance in what is now Tokyo Bay. Thus, like maguro (tuna), kohada (gizzard shad), and anago (conger eel), it is a part of classic Edo-style sushi. Jiro Ono says, ***"Because clams become tough quickly when cooked, we place it on the fire for just a short time. We then steep it in broth, to which we add seasoning like sugar and soy sauce to adjust the flavor."*** Sweet, juicy hamaguri is a perfect match with vinegared rice.

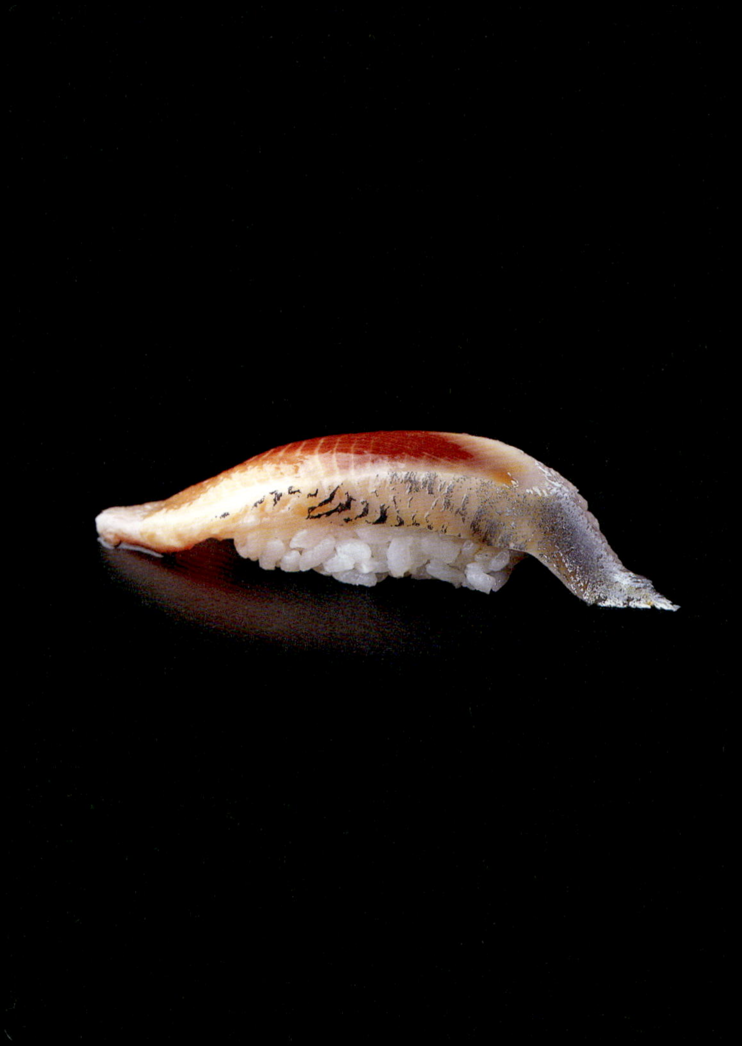

SUKIYABASHI JIRO's Tasting Menu 22

いわし

Iwashi : Sardine

【鰯】 6月から10月：June - October

　いわしは下魚などと呼ばれているが『次郎』のおまかせメニューでは、まぐろやえびのあとに握られて出てくる。小野二郎は言う。「夏からのいわしは脂が乗っていて、まぐろに負けません。ただし、足が速いので、築地から買ってくると、真っ先に手をつけます。冷たい氷水の中で内臓を取り出し、劣化を最小限にとどめるようにします。この手当を素早くやることが肝心です。握ったらすぐに召し上がってください。そのまま置いておくとすぐに生臭みが出てきます」

Iwashi has been called a cheap fish. At Sukiyabashi Jiro, however, it comes after maguro (tuna) or ebi (prawn) in our omakase tasting menu. Jiro Ono says, *"Iwashi becomes fatty from summer, and rivals maguro in richness. But because it spoils quickly, we immediately prepare it when it is brought in from Tsukiji Market. We remove its innards in ice water to minimize its deterioration. Working quickly is crucial. Please eat iwashi as soon as it is served. If you leave it sitting, it will quickly develop an unpleasant odor."*

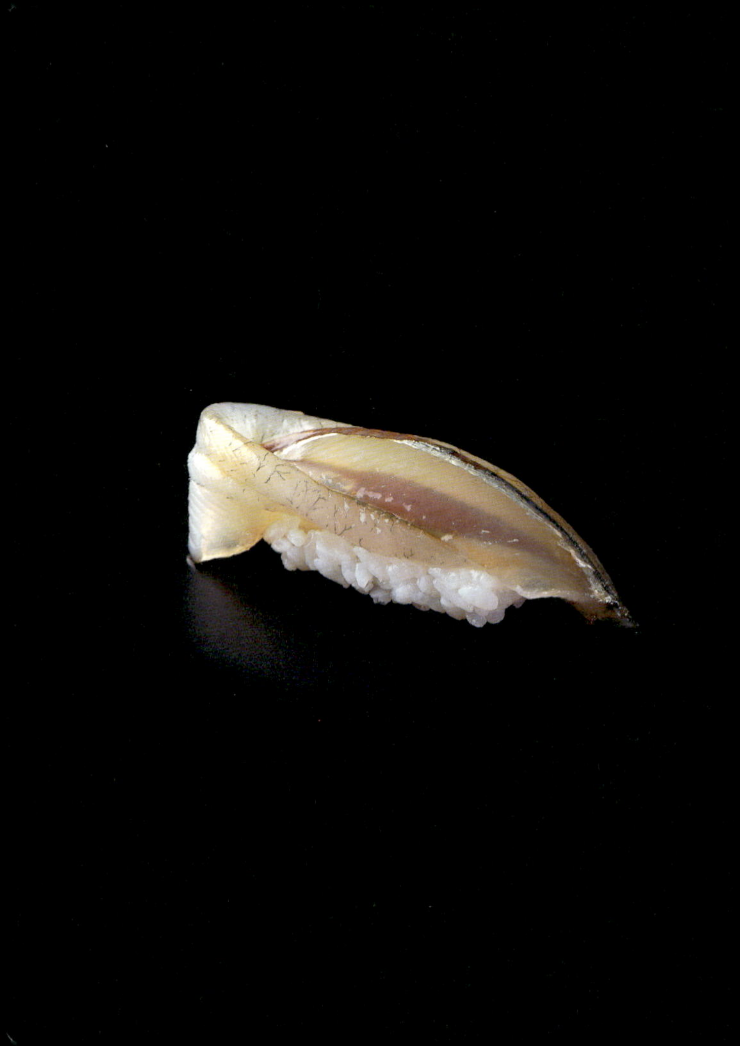

SUKIYABASHI JIRO's Tasting Menu

さより

Sayori : Halfbeak

【細魚】 11月から3月 : November - March

　さよりは鮨屋では、白身ではなく、ひかりものに入る。脂の乗ったさよりは舌の上を滑るような、透明感のある旨みを感じさせる魚である。小野二郎は言う。「昔は〈細魚〉と書くように、細めのさよりでも脂が乗ったのがあったので、ひねって握ったんですが、最近は太いのが多くて、ひねることができなくなりました」。一時、いわしが不漁のときには出番が多かったのだが、最近また、いわしが豊漁になってくると、さよりが品書きに載る機会が少なくなってきている。

For sushi chefs, sayori is not considered a whitefish but rather a silver-skinned fish. It has a clear flavor, and glides on your tongue because of its fattiness. Jiro Ono says, *"As its past nickname 'needlefish' suggests, sayori is thin. We would twist two together and place them on top of sushi rice. Recently, there have been many plump sayori, so we can't twist them anymore."* For a while, sayori was served often because of poor catches of iwashi (sardine). However, because iwashi are now abundant, the opportunity for sayori to appear on the menu has become limited.

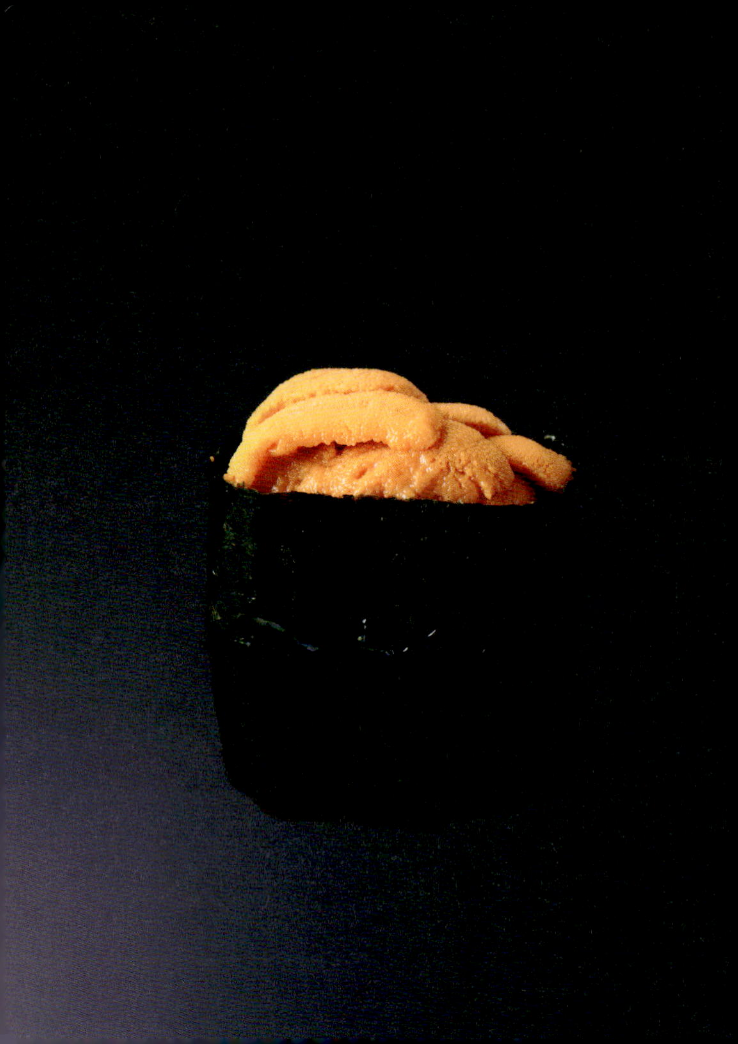

SUKIYABASHI JIRO's Tasting Menu 24

うに
Uni : Sea Urchin

【雲丹】 通年：All seasons

『次郎』のうにの鮨を頬張って、「まるでクリームを食べているみたいだ」と絶賛したのが、フランス料理のマエストロ、ジョエル・ロブションである。北海道産のうにを使うが、毎朝、炭であぶった香り高いのりを合わせるところが、他店と大きく違うところ。二郎は言う。「うにを山盛りにしてますが、一口で頬張ると、うにとのりと酢めしがいいバランスでひとつになるんです」

When he placed Sukiyabashi Jiro's uni sushi in his mouth, the French maestro Joël Robuchon exclaimed, *"It's as if I'm eating cream."* Sukiyabashi Jiro procures uni grown in Hokkaido. We roll it with nori (seaweed) grilled over coals every morning, a practice that sets Sukiyabashi Jiro apart from other sushi restaurants. Jiro Ono says, *"I heap uni on rice so that when you place the entire sushi in your mouth, the uni and nori and vinegared rice balance and become one."*

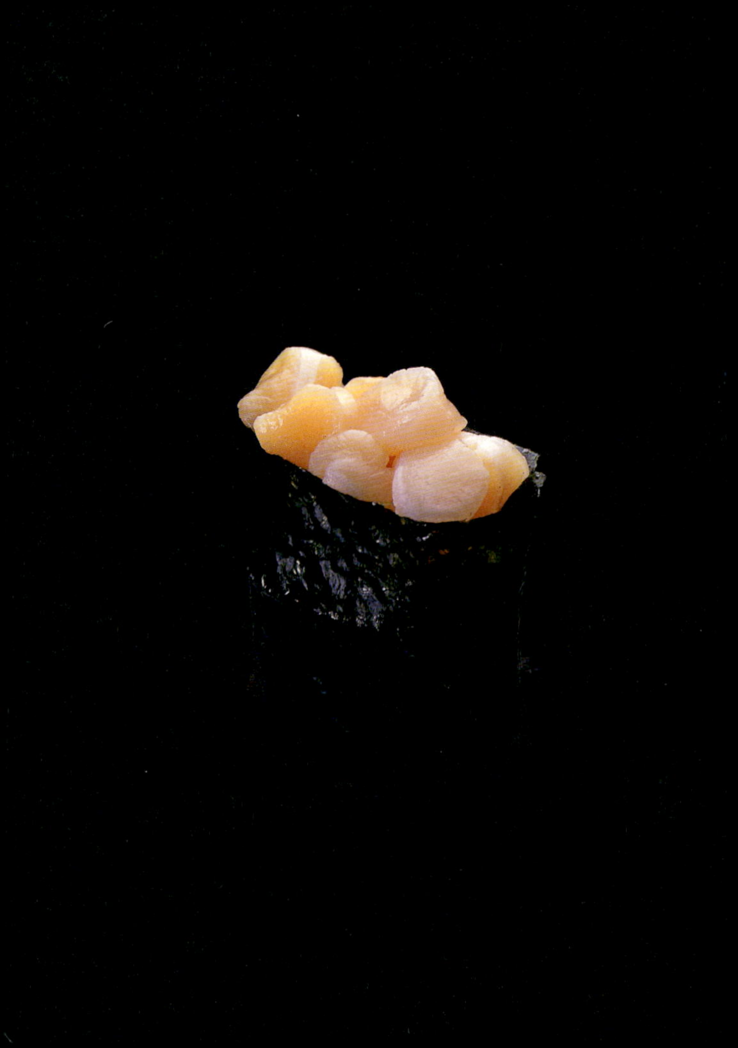

SUKIYABASHI JIRO's Tasting Menu 25

こばしら

Kobashira : Mactra Adductor Muscle

【小柱】 通年：All seasons

　こばしらは、ばか貝の柱だが、『次郎』のこばしらは名前とは違って大きくて立派な貝柱である。「おまかせ」の後半、うに、いくらと並んで軍艦巻きで登場する。二郎は言う。「うちではのりを毎朝あぶっていますが、そののりととても相性がいいんです。でも、最近、大粒のものが手に入りにくくなってきました。一説には、近々、なくなるかもしれないと。今のうちにしっかりと味を覚えといてください」

Kobashira is the adductor muscle of mactra clams. At Sukiyabashi Jiro, our kobashira differs from what is typically offered by other sushi restaurants – its size is stupendous. For the latter half of our omakase tasting menu, kobashira makes its appearance in a *"warship roll"* after uni (sea urchin) and ikura (salmon roe). Jiro says, *"We roast our seaweed every morning. Kobashira matches its flavor perfectly. These days, however, it's been tough getting our hands on large kobashira. These clams may disappear in the near future. Be sure to try kobashira soon and savor its taste."*

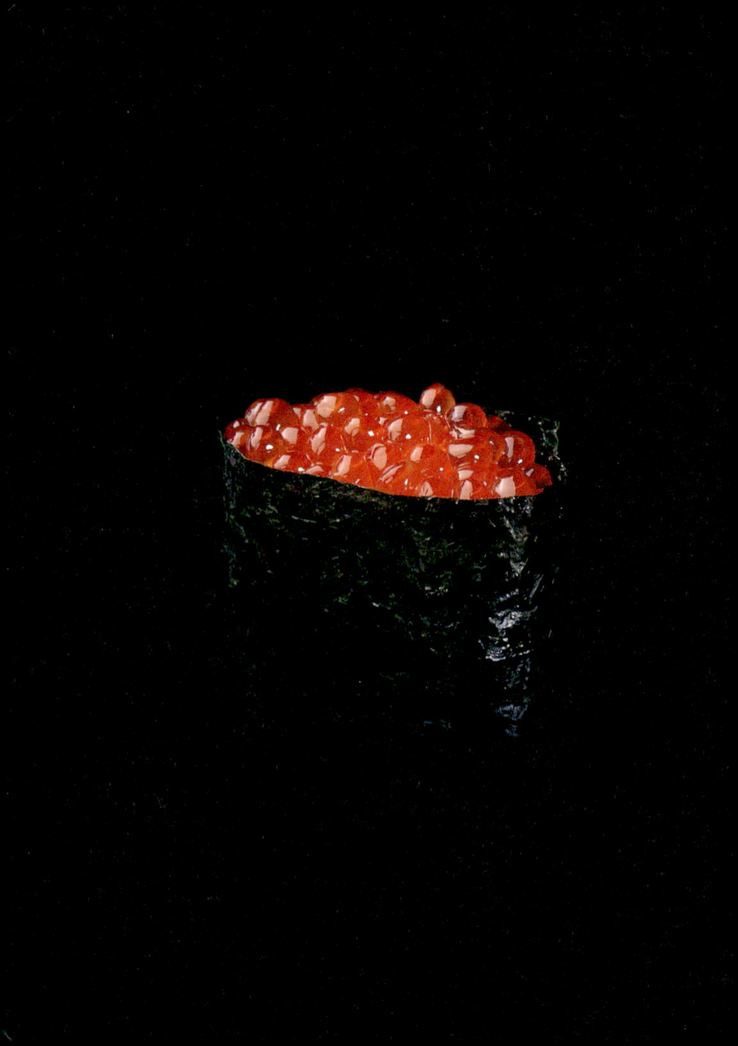

SUKIYABASHI JIRO's Tasting Menu 26

いくら

Ikura : Salmon Roe

【イクラ】 通年：All seasons

『次郎』では、築地では酢めしと合う、活けの魚しか仕入れてこない。養殖の魚、冷凍の魚介は一切扱わない。そのなかにあって、唯一、例外がある。それがいくらである。小野二郎いわく、「いくらを秋の旬だけではなく一年中出せないかと、冷凍にすることを考えました。うちのはいくらの醤油漬けなんですが、魚卵を鶏卵のように仕立ててあり、卵かけごはんみたいと言われたときは嬉しかったですね」。

At Sukiyabashi Jiro, we only procure fish that goes well with vinegared rice: fish delivered chilled from Tsukiji Market with their quality and freshness maintained. We never use farmed fish or frozen fish. There is only one exception to this rule: ikura. Jiro Ono says, *"Ikura is produced by salmon only once a year, in the fall. Because of this, we decided to use frozen ikura so we can serve it year-round. We marinate ikura in soy sauce. Our ikura have a smooth texture and mild taste on par with fresh chicken eggs. I'm very happy when customers tell me that our ikura sushi is like raw eggs over rice."*

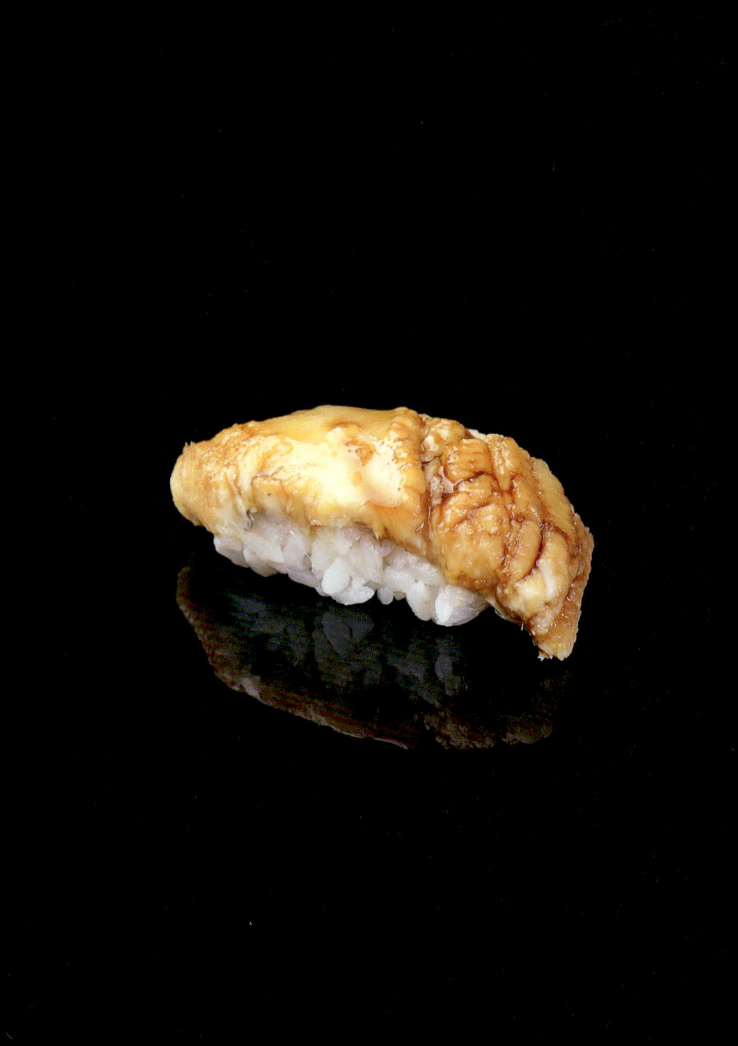

SUKIYABASHI JIRO's Tasting Menu

あなご
Anago : Conger Eel

【穴子】 通年：All seasons

　小野二郎いわく「とても柔らかく煮上げてありますから、握るのがむずかしい。ひょっとすると、あなごがいちばんむずかしいかもしれません。握るときは、あなごの上からはほとんど力を加えていません、力を入れているように見えても、さわっているだけです（笑）」。『次郎』では、煮上げた段階で調理が完結しているから、よその鮨屋がよくやるように、握る際にあぶったりはしない。

Jiro Ono says, *"Because we cook anago to be very tender, serving it in sushi is very difficult. It is perhaps the most difficult sushi to prepare. When shaping the sushi, you can't place any force on top of the anago."* Jiro laughs. *"Even if it looks like we're using strength, we're merely touching it."* At Sukiyabashi Jiro, our anago is perfectly finished when it is simmered. Unlike other sushi restaurants, we don't broil it further when preparing its sushi.

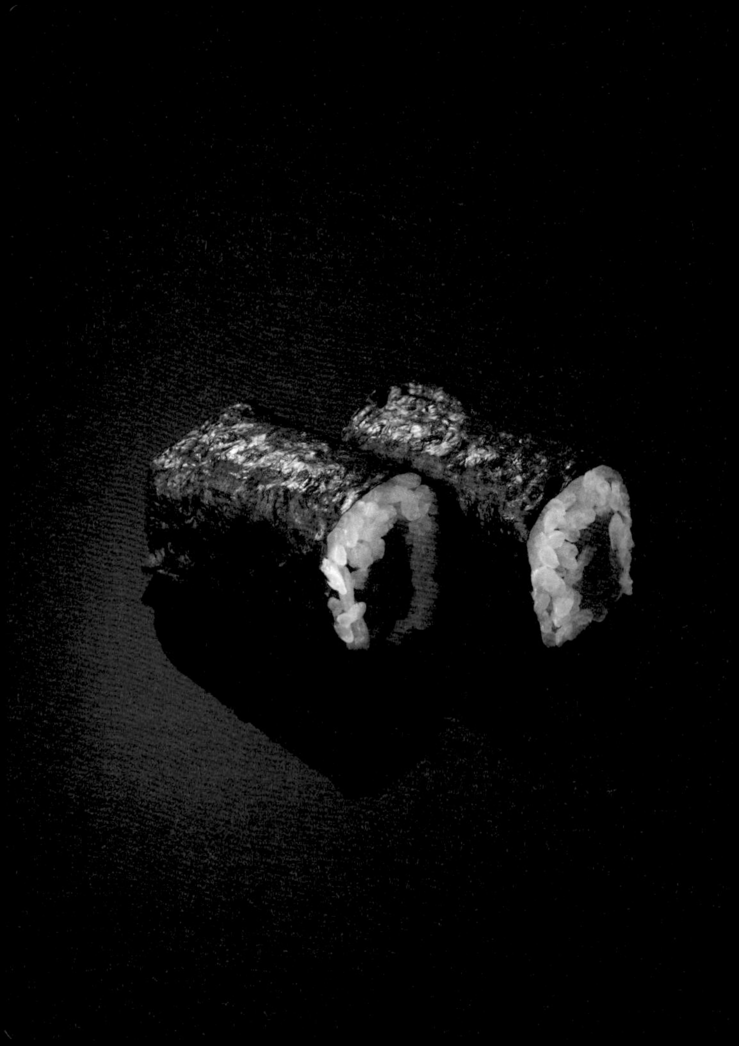

SUKIYABASHI JIRO's Tasting Menu 28

かんぴょう巻き

Kanpyo-Maki : Dried Shavings of Calabash Gourd

【干瓢巻】 通年：All seasons

　かんぴょうののり巻きは「おまかせ」のメニューにはなく、お客の注文があると「あなご」の後に巻いてくれる。小野二郎は言う。「以前はかんぴょうを用意していてもほとんど注文がありませんでした。ところが、お薦めしてるうちに人気が出てきて、いまでは始終かんぴょうを煮ています。うちが日本でいちばんのり巻きを巻いているんじゃないでしょうか。昔のようにいいかんぴょうがなかなか手に入らないのが残念です」

Sukiyabashi Jiro's kanpyo-maki rolled with seaweed is not part of our omakase tasting menu. But we serve it after anago (conger eel) upon customers' request. Jiro Ono says, *"In the past, we prepared kanpyo, but almost no one ordered it. But as we recommended it, it became popular. Nowadays, we cook kanpyo all day long. I wouldn't be surprised if we make the most kanpyo-maki in Japan. It's unfortunate that you can't get good kanpyo as in the past."*

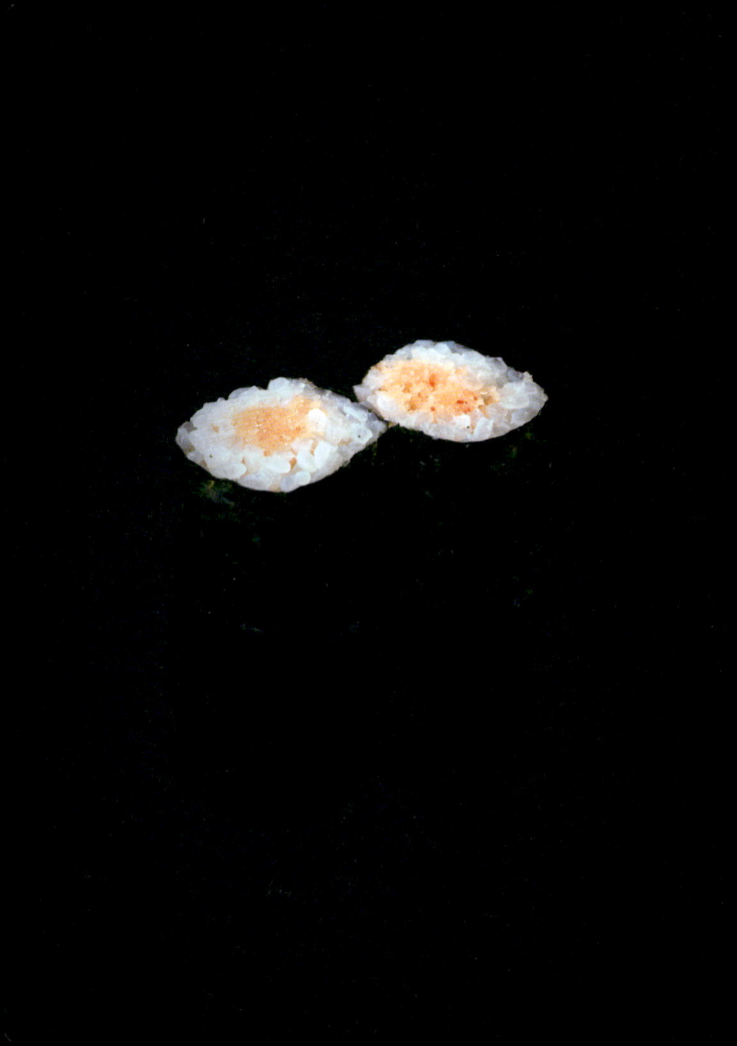

SUKIYABASHI JIRO's Tasting Menu 29

おぼろ

Oboro

【朧】 通年：All seasons

「おぼろ」は、ちらしには欠かせない鮨種だが、現在、『すきやばし次郎』では、ちらしを作らないので、注文に応じて巻物にする。『次郎』のおぼろは芝えびだけを丹念に摺ってつくったもの。小野二郎は言う。「面倒と思わずに手間をかければ、美味しくなるのが、おぼろです」

Oboro is an essential topping for chirashi (vinegared rice served with various colorful toppings of seafood, vegetables, and egg). However, because currently we don't make chirashi at Sukiyabashi Jiro, we serve oboro upon request in rolled sushi. Our oboro is made exclusively from minced prawn. Jiro Ono says, *"Oboro is delicious if you take time to make it."*

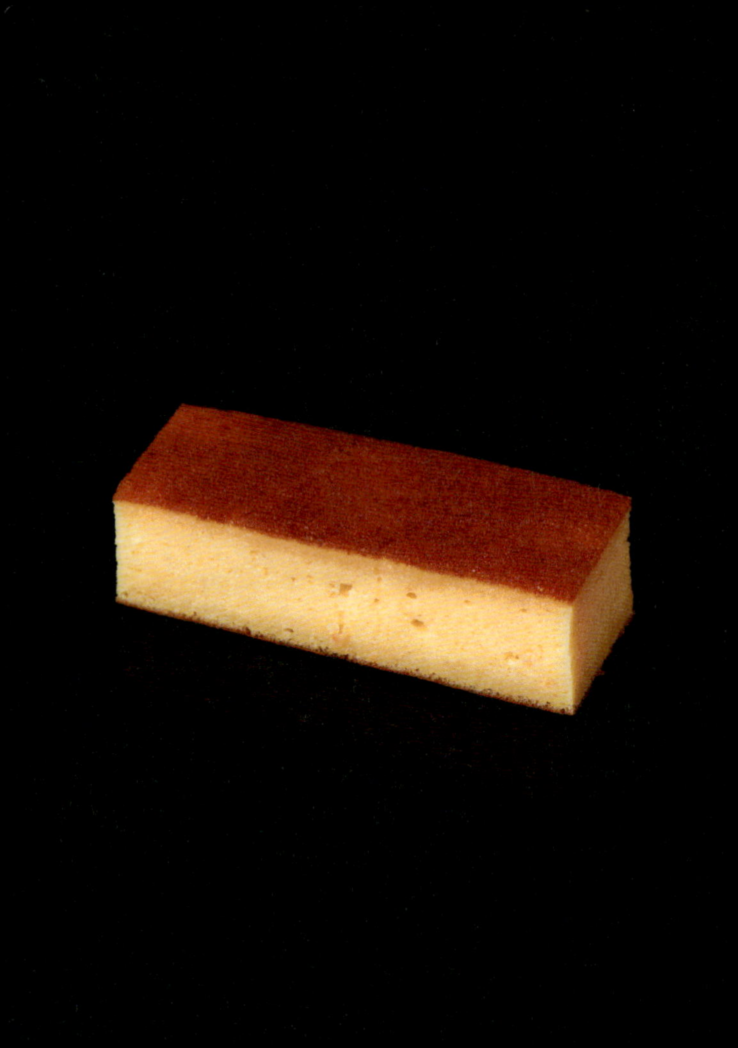

SUKIYABASHI JIRO's Tasting Menu 30

たまご

Tamago : Grilled Eggs

【玉子】 通年：All seasons

「おまかせ」メニューの掉尾を飾るのがたまご。外国の方は「オムレット」と呼ぶ人もいる。小野二郎は言う。「うちではこれが焼けるようになったら、職人として一人前です。玉子のほか大和芋、海老がふんだんに入っています。1枚焼くのに約1時間かかります。かつては、酢めしと一緒に握ってお出ししてたのですが、『おまかせ』でたくさんにぎりを召し上がられた後なので、いまはそのままデザートのようにお出ししています」

Tamago, called *"omelette"* by some of our international customers, is the final offering of our omakase tasting menu. Jiro Ono says, *"At Sukiyabashi Jiro, a sign of a professional chef is the ability to cook tamago. Besides eggs, we usually also mix in yamato-imo (Japanese yam) and shrimp. Grilling just one tamago takes about an hour. In the past, we served tamago on top of vinegared rice as sushi. But since our customers enjoy many sushi toppings as part of our omakase, we now simply serve tamago by itself, like a dessert."*

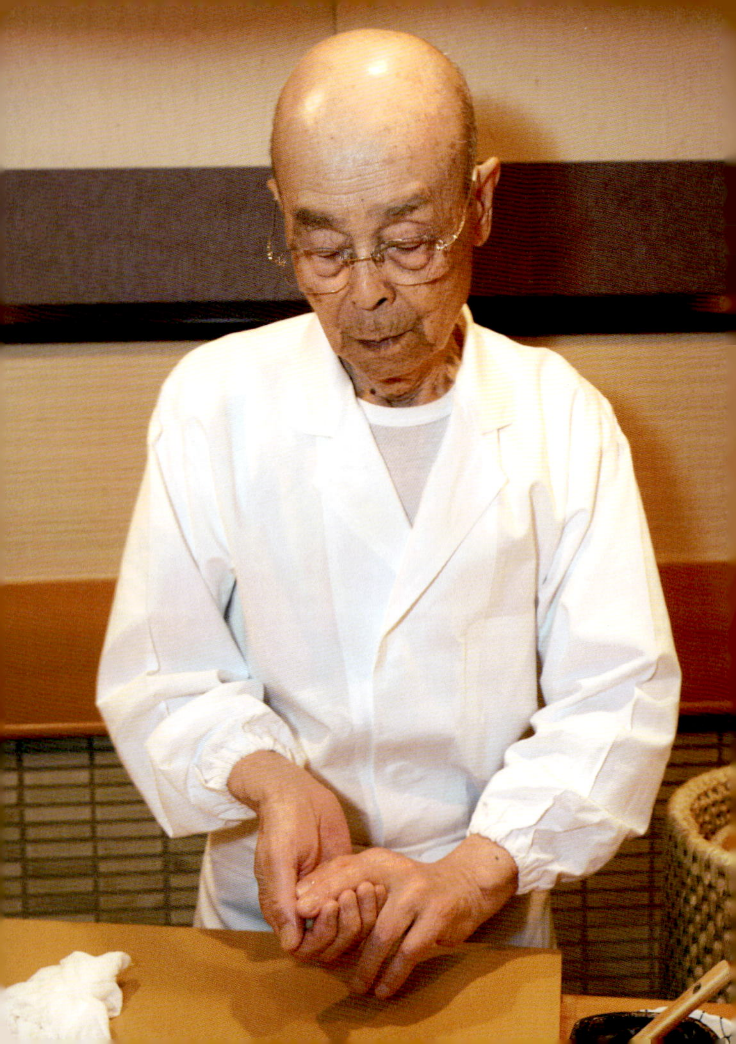

CHAPTER 2

鮨を美味しく食べる

Eating Recipe

はじめに

　にぎりずしは手でつまんでも、箸を使って食べても、どちらでも構いません。
『すきやばし次郎』の箸は、両端が細くなっている、いわゆる利休箸と呼ばれるもの。片方を使えば、もう一方は神様が使う箸先ということになります。長さは７寸５分、約23センチ。肘をついて手首までの長さで、江戸時代に決められた由緒ある寸法です。これを２本つなげると１尺５寸となり、てんぷらを揚げる箸はこの長さで竹でできています。「箸」が竹かんむりに者と書く由縁です。鮨もてんぷらも３尺挟んで職人と客が向かい合います。握りたての鮨や揚げたてのてんぷらを出すのに程よい距離で、互いに息苦しくもありません。この絶妙の間合いを挟んで向かい合うのが「江戸前」の屋台で発達を遂げてきた料理の本来の姿です。鮨屋やてんぷら屋のカウンターでは、酌み交わす酒や賑やかなおしゃべりは不必要、むしろ禁物。酒や会話を楽しみたいのなら、テーブル席へどうぞ、と願います。

山本益博

Introduction

It doesn't matter if you pick up sushi with your fingers or with chopsticks. At Sukiyabashi Jiro, the chopsticks are tapered on both ends. This type of chopsticks is called *"rikyubashi."* It is said that when you use one end, God uses the other. The chopsticks' length is 7-sun-5-bu, or roughly 23 centimeters. It is about the length from one's elbow to wrist, and served as a traditional unit of measure developed in the Edo era. Two of these units make 1-shaku-5-sun, which is the length of chopsticks used to cook tempura. Tempura chopsticks are made of bamboo. That is why the kanji character for chopsticks, or *"hashi"* (箸), is written using characters of a *"person"* (者) under *"bamboo"* (竹). The sushi or tempura chef and the customer face each other with a distance of three shaku in between. This is just the right distance for serving freshly made sushi or fried tempura. The distance also promotes a congenial atmosphere between the chef and customer without being smothering. This finely tuned distance lies at the foundation of cuisine originating from Edo-era food stalls. At a sushi or tempura counter, there is no need to trade banter while drinking or dining together; in fact, it is taboo. If you wish to chat and enjoy conversation, please sit at a table.

Masuhiro Yamamoto

その1 手でつまむ

　小野二郎の握る鮨はごく軽く握られているため、空気をいっぱい含んでいて、黒板(くろいた)に置かれたとき、軟着陸します。これをつまむのは容易ではありません。酢めしの両端をつかむのではなく、そーっとつまみあげると形が崩れません。

1. Pick it up with your fingers

Because Jiro Ono makes sushi with an extremely light touch, it contains a lot of air. When it is placed on your plate, it lands softly. It is not easy to hold. Don't pick it up by both ends. Gently lift it up so that it maintains its shape.

その2 箸でつかむ

　黒板に置かれたにぎりずしを箸でつかむ場合は、にぎりを神輿に見立てて、その黒板に沿って箸を担ぎ棒のように渡し、両脇からそーっと持ち上げるようにしてつかみます。箸でにぎりを斜めに持ち上げようとすると、必ず酢めしが崩れ落ちます。

2. Pick it up with your chopsticks

If you wish to pick up the sushi placed on your tray with a pair of chopsticks, think of the sushi as a portable shrine. Place your chopsticks parallel to the tray as if they are the shrine's carrying poles, and lift up the sushi by grasping it along its sides. If you grasp it through its middle with your chopsticks, it will surely fall apart.

その3 すし種を落とさず食べる

　鮨を持つときに、上からかぶせるように持ち上げると、鮨種を軽くトッピングしている軍艦巻きなどは、口に運ぶときに鮨種が落ちてしまうことがあります。そっと持ち上げて、そのまま一口でいただきましょう。

3. Avoid spilling the sushi topping

If you pick up a battleship roll sushi from above with your fingers, the sushi topping will fall out when you transport the sushi to your mouth. Instead, lift up the sushi gently by grasping its sides, and eat the entire sushi in one bite.

その4 醤油をつける

　もし、にぎりに「煮切り醤油」がすし職人の怠慢で引かれていなかったら、しょうがを少量つまんで刷毛替わりに使い、それを醤油に浸してから、すし種の上に引きましょう。
　にぎりをつまんでから醤油をつけるのは至難の業です。

4. Flavor it with soy sauce

If, by chance, the sushi chef has neglected to brush nikiri shoyu on your sushi, pick up a small amount of shoga (pickled ginger) to use as a substitute for the brush. Soak it in soy sauce, and then brush it across the top of the sushi topping. It is next to impossible to pick up sushi to dip into soy sauce.

その5 しょうがをつまむ

5. Eat some shoga

　しょうがはにぎりの味を切る役目をしますが、食べすぎると口の中が辛くなるばかりです。要所を考えていただきましょう。

Shoga (pickled ginger) cleanses your palate. But too much of it will burn your mouth. Eat a pinch to remove the aftertaste of fat.

その6 お茶を飲む

6. Drink tea

「鮨の後味を切るには、お茶が一番」というのが小野二郎の持論。『次郎』のお茶は熱いのでお水もお出ししています。

To cleanse the palate of an aftertaste, Jiro Ono believes that drinking tea is best. Water is also available for guests who consider tea too hot.

その7　醤油に浸さない
7. Don't dip sushi rice into soy sauce

酢めしに醤油をつけると、酢めしの味が台無しになります。

If you dip sushi rice in soy sauce, you will spoil its flavor.

その8　甘いつめに辛い醤油をつけない
8. Sweet tsume sauce

甘いつめが塗られた鮨に醤油をつける必要はありません。

You don't need to add soy sauce to sushi already flavored with tsume sauce.

その9 にぎりをひっくり返さない
9. Don't turn nigiri sushi upside down

酢めしが人肌の温度なのは、舌に違和感がないためです。

If you turn sushi upside down when eating it, your mouth will feel a strange sensation since the rice has a temperature different from your tongue.

その10 すし種をはがして食べない
10. Don't separate the sushi topping

すし種をはがすのは、職人仕事の最大の侮辱です。

Pulling off the topping is the greatest insult to the sushi chef.

その11 ふたつにちぎって食べない
11. Don't break sushi into two

にぎりは一口サイズで2寸5分、舌先は3寸です。
A piece of sushi fits into your mouth. Its size is roughly 6 centimeters long.

その12 鮨をためない
12. Don't let sushi sit

鮨は握りたてが、なによりいちばん美味しいです。
There is nothing more delicious than sushi that has just been placed on your plate.

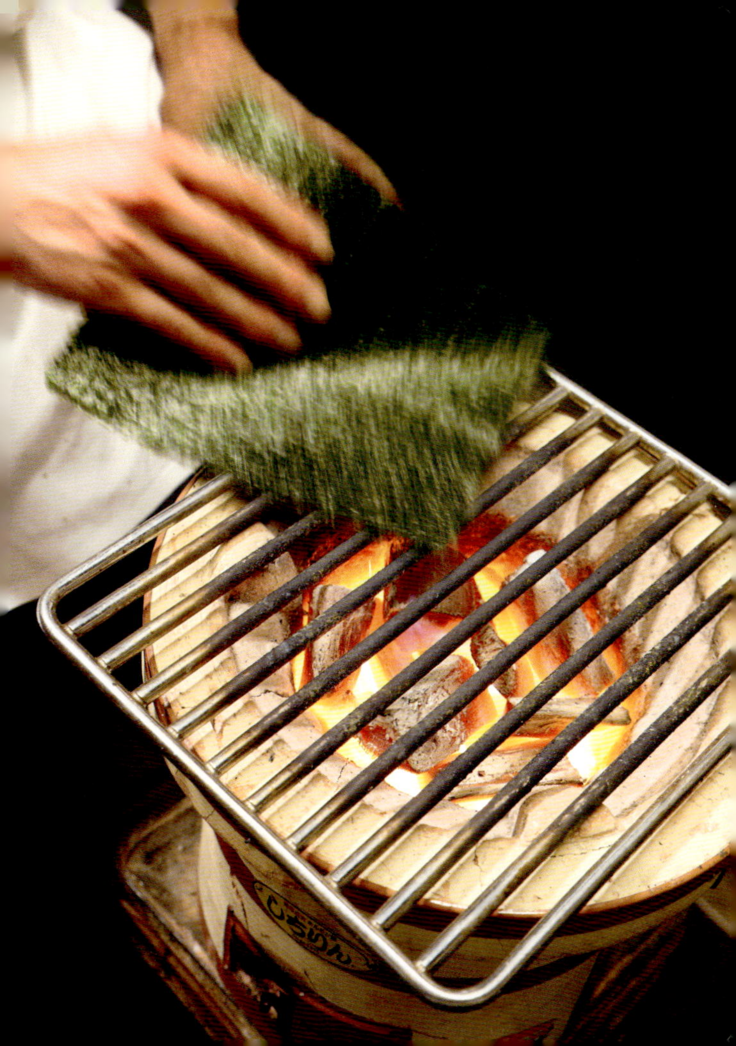
しちりん

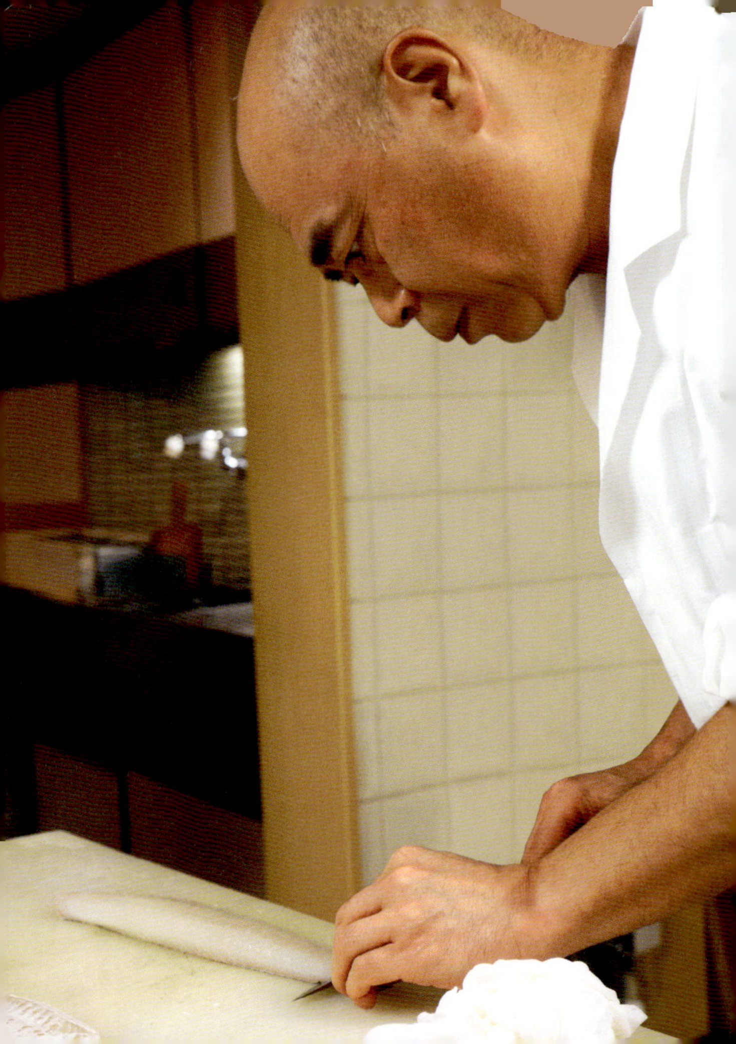

CHAPTER 3

すきやばし次郎の
トリセツ

Dining at Jiro

予約

Reservations

『すきやばし次郎』では毎月1日（日曜、1月を除く）朝9時から翌月分の予約を受け付けています。外国のお客様は、まずホテルを予約し、コンシェルジュに『すきやばし次郎』の予約を依頼する方が多くいらっしゃいます。外国語での電話の応対はしていません。おひとり様の予約をされる方がいらっしゃいますが、小野二郎は鮨を握るピッチが速く、それに追いつけない方が多いようです。『すきやばし次郎』のにぎりずしを楽しむのでしたら、ふたり以上で出かけることをお薦めいたします。

Sukiyabashi Jiro accepts reservations from 9 a.m. of the first day (except Sunday) of each month (except January) for the following month. Many of our international guests ask their hotels' concierges to make reservations for them. Regrettably, we cannot answer phone calls in a language other than Japanese. We welcome single diners. However, Jiro Ono serves sushi at a quick pace, and many single diners cannot keep up. To fully enjoy sushi at Sukiyabashi Jiro, we recommend a party of two or more guests.

店を訪れる

Arriving at Sukiyabashi Jiro

　予約時間は厳守して、遅れないようにしましょう。予約の時間に合わせて、ご飯を炊き上げ、酢めしを用意しているので、時間に遅れると、『すきやばし次郎』のにぎりずしを存分に楽しめなくなります。店はカウンター席10席のみです。『すきやばし次郎』では築地から、にぎりの酢めしに合う魚介しか仕入れてこないため、酒のつまみの用意はありません。『次郎』のお薦めは、お茶です。鮨の写真をとるのは遠慮しましょう。にぎりを食べることに集中したほうが、『次郎』のにぎりを楽しめること請け合いです。帰り際、手が空いてさえすれば、玄関先で記念撮影に応じます。

Observe the reservation time, and try not to be late. Because we cook rice and prepare vinegared rice based on your reservation time, if you are late, you won't be able to enjoy Sukiyabashi Jiro's sushi to the fullest. The restaurant only has ten counter seats. Since we procure sea food daily from Tsukiji that complements the taste of sushi rice, we do not have snacks to serve with saké. Jiro's recommended beverage is green tea. Please refrain from taking photos of the sushi. The only sure way of enjoying Jiro's sushi is to concentrate on dining. When you leave, we would be pleased to take a commemorative photograph for you at the doorway if you wish.

すきやばし 次郎

「おまかせ」を食べる

Enjoying Our Omakase Tasting Menu

　現在、『すきやばし次郎』では、献立は「おまかせコース」のにぎりのみです。すべてのお客様に小野二郎がすしを握ります。カウンターに置かれている「おまかせ」の品書きは、当日、朝、にぎりの順番が決められ、作られたものです。約20貫あります。かなりのボリュームですが、小野二郎は、年配の女性のお客様には、はじめから小さめに握る配慮をしています。にぎりが目の前にある黒板（くろいた）の上に置かれたら、すぐに召し上がってください。握り終わった状態が、いちばん美味しい状態に仕上げてあるからです。にぎりには煮切り醬油が引かれてあるので、小皿の醬油をにぎりにつける必要はありません。

Right now, at Sukiyabashi Jiro we serve only the omakase tasting menu. Jiro Ono makes the sushi for all customers. The omakase tasting menu served at the counter is determined in the morning each day and served in order. It consists of about 20 sushi pieces. That is quite a large amount. However, Jiro Ono takes care to make each piece smaller for older women customers. Please eat the sushi soon after it is placed on the plate in front of you. Its flavors are at their most exquisite when the sushi has just been prepared. Because "nikiri" soy sauce has already been brushed on the sushi, there is no need to dip it in a saucer of soy sauce.

ドレスコード

Dress code

　ドレスコードは特別に設けていませんが、ほとんどのお客はジャケットを着用しています。襟なしのシャツ、半ズボン、サンダルの方は入店をお断りする場合があります。また、香水は控えめにお願いいたします。背もたれにバッグを置かずに、預けましょう。

Sukiyabashi Jiro has no special dress code. Many guests wear jackets. We may, however, refuse service to customers wearing collarless shirts or shorts, or sandals. We ask our guests to refrain from wearing strong perfume. Please hand over your bag for safekeeping instead of slinging it over a chair.

支払い

Payment

　以前は、支払いは現金のみでしたが、現在はクレジットカードが使えるようになりました。お支払いは、「おまかせコース」は昼夜ともに同じく30000円プラス消費税です。

In the past, only cash was accepted, but now you can also pay by credit card. The cost of the omakase tasting menu is 30,000 yen plus tax for either lunch or dinner.

次郎

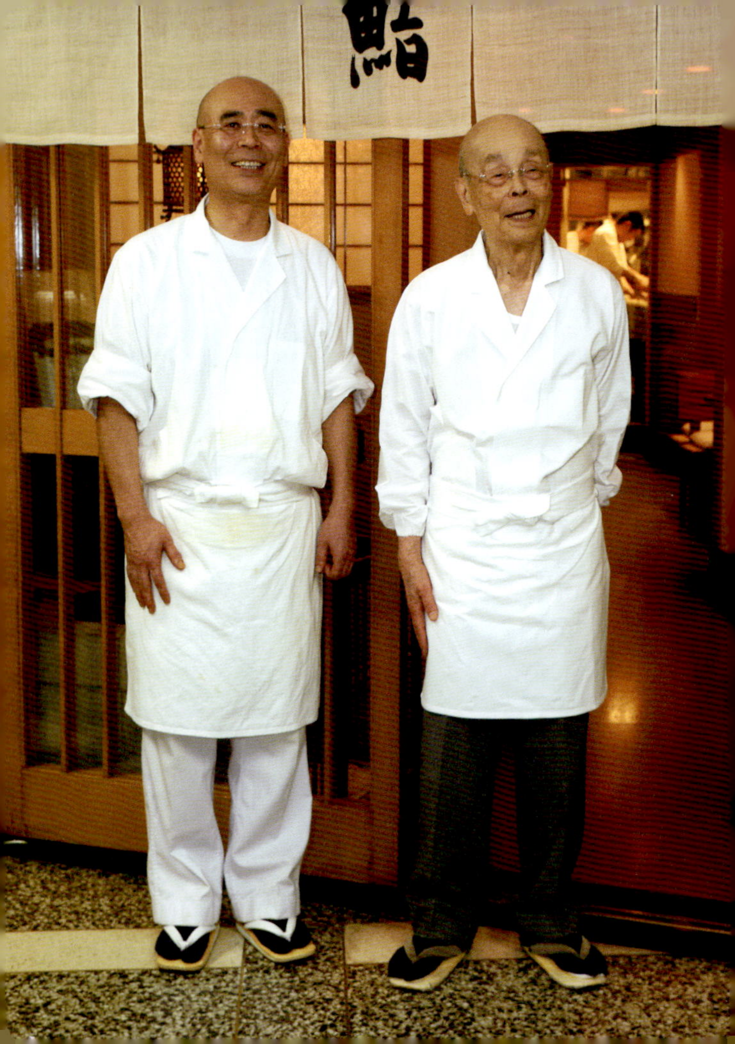
鮨

見送り

Visiting Sukiyabashi Jiro again

『すきやばし次郎』は観光名所ではありません。季節が違えば、夏なら「かつお」、冬なら「さば」といった具合に、すし種が変わります。一度訪れて気に入られたら、ぜひとも、再び、足を運んでみてください。訪れるたびに『すきやばし次郎』の良さがわかるはずです。

Dining at Sukiyabashi Jiro is not like visiting a tourist attraction. Different seasons bring different sushi. If you have enjoyed your experience at Sukiyabashi Jiro, be sure to come again. Each visit will bring new discoveries.

すきやばし次郎
住所：東京都中央区銀座４－２－１５　塚本素山ビル B1
電話：０３－３５３５－３６００
営業時間：１１：３０～１４：００、１７：３０～２０：３０

Sukiyabashi Jiro
Tsukamoto Sozan Building Basement, 4-2-15 Ginza, Chuo-ku, Tokyo, Japan
Tel: 03-3535-3600 (+81-3-3535-3600 from abroad), Business hours: 11:30 a.m. to 2 p.m., 5:30 p.m. to 8 p.m.

すきやばし次郎　六本木店
住所：東京都港区六本木６－１２－２
電話：０３－５４１３－６６２６
営業時間：１１：３０～１４：００、１７：３０～２１：００

Sukiyabashi Jiro Roppongi
6-12-2 Roppongi, Minato-ku, Tokyo, Japan, Tel: 03-5413-6626 (+81-3-5413-6626 from abroad), Business hours: 11:30 a.m. to 2 p.m., 5:30 p.m. to 9 p.m.

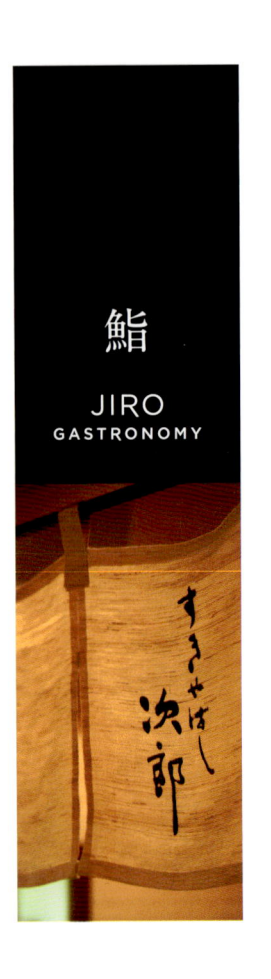

著者：小野二郎、小野禎一
監修：山本益博

撮影：管洋志、泉健太
デザイン：宮坂 淳
翻訳：リングァ・ギルド
編集：尾崎 靖（小学館）、小野綾子（小学館）
プリンティング・ディレクション：
　　　　野口啓一（凸版グラフィックアーツ）
協力：すきやばし次郎、管洋介、Haruna Eto

2014年　9月17日　　第1版第1刷発行
2023年　2月6日　　　　第9刷発行

著作者　　小野二郎、山本益博
発行者　　大澤竜二
発行所　　株式会社 小学館
　　　　　東京都千代田区一ツ橋2-3-1 〒101-8001
　　　　　編集：03-3230-5707 **販売**：03-5281-3555
DTP　　　株式会社昭和ブライト
印刷所　　凸版印刷株式会社
製本所　　牧製本印刷株式会社

造本には十分注意しておりますが、印刷、製本などの製造上の不備がございましたら「制作局コールセンター」（フリーダイヤル0120-336-340）にご連絡ください。電話受付は、土・日・祝休日を除く9:30～17:30。本書の無断での複写（コピー）、上演、放送等の二次利用、翻案等は、著作権法上の例外を除き禁じられています。本書の電子データ化などの無断複製は、著作権法上の例外を除き、禁じられています。代行業者等の第三者による電子的複製も認められておりません。

©JIRO ONO, MASUHIRO YAMAMOTO
2014 Printed in Japan　ISBN978-4-09-388385-6